Created in Christ

a Junior High Bible Study Collection

Concordia Publishing House

Copyright © 2006 Concordia Publishing House
3558 S. Jefferson Ave., St. Louis, MO 63118-3968
1-800-325-3040 • www.cph.org

All rights reserved. Unless specifically noted, no part of this publication may be reproduced, stored in a retrieval system, or transmitted, in any form or by any means, electronic, mechanical, photocopying, recording, or otherwise, without the prior written permission of Concordia Publishing House.

The purchaser of this publication is allowed to reproduce the marked portions contained herein for classroom use. These resources may not be transferred or copied to another user.

Portions originally published by Concordia Publishing House, copyright © 1999, 2000, 2001, 2002, 2003, 2004.

Written by Kurt Bickel, Tom Couser, Daniel Czapleski, Christopher Drager, Nicole Dreyer, Bianca Elliott, Jim Elsner, Gretchen Gebhardt, Rich Gutekunst, Barrie Henke, Timothy Klinkenberg, Naomi Low, Glen Lucas, Kurt Mews, Max Murphy, William Ney, Beth Orstadt, Daniel Pfaffe, Jay Reed, Greg Rommel, Christine Ross, Byron Schroeder, Ted Schroeder, Julie Stiegemeyer, Cynthia Twillman, Susan Voss, Malinda Walz, and Cynthia Werner.

Edited by Mark Sengele

Scripture quotations are taken from the HOLY BIBLE, NEW INTERNATIONAL VERSION®. NIV®. Copyright © 1973, 1978, 1984 by International Bible Society. Used by permission of Zondervan Publishing House. All rights reserved.

Your comments and suggestions concerning the material are appreciated. Please write to the Editor of Youth Materials, Concordia Publishing House, 3558 S. Jefferson Avenue, St. Louis, MO 63118-3968.

This publication may be available in braille, in large print, or on cassette tape for the visually impaired. Please allow 8 to 12 weeks for delivery. Write to the Library for the Blind, 7550 Watson Rd., St. Louis, MO 63119-4409; call toll-free 1-888-215-2455; or visit the Web site: www.blindmission.org.

Manufactured in the United States of America

1 2 3 4 5 6 7 8 9 10   15 14 13 12 11 10 09 08 07 06

Table of Contents

Lesson	Title	Bible Story	Page
1	**Life Giving**	God Creates the World	6
2	**A Precious Gift**	God Creates Adam and Eve	8
3	**The Blame Game**	The Fall into Sin	10
4	**God's Attitude**	Cain and Abel	12
5	**By Faith**	Noah and the Flood	14
6	**Saved by Faith!**	God Calls Abram	16
7	**Do You Trust Me?**	Abraham and Isaac	18
8	**Telling His Story**	Rebekah and Isaac	20
9	**God's Blessings**	Jacob and Esau	22
10	**Bad That Works for Good**	Joseph's Dreams	24
11	**Heart Check**	Joseph Reconciles with Brothers	26
12	**God's Calling**	Birth and Call of Moses	28
13	**God Passes Over**	Passover	30
14	**Great Escapes**	Crossing the Red Sea	32
15	**Improper Prayers**	God Provides Manna/Quail	34
16	**The Road Trip**	Israelites in the Wilderness	36
17	**Letting God Lead**	Israelites and the Promised Land	38
18	**Foreigner No More**	The Story of Ruth	40
19	**Giving Back to God**	Hannah and Samuel	42
20	**God's Patience**	Saul Becomes King	44
21	**Step-by-Step**	David Is Anointed King	46
22	**Real Friendship**	David and Jonathan	48
23	**Cleaning Up Your Act**	David and Bathsheba	50
24	**God's House**	Solomon Builds the Temple	52
25	**Victory!**	Elijah and the Priest of Baal	54
26	**Something So Simple**	Naaman Healed of Leprosy	56

Lesson	Title	Bible Story	Page
27	**Spiritual Sickness**	Joash Rules over Judah	58
28	**Promises and Trust**	Hezekiah Rules over Judah	60
29	**Preparing for God's Play**	The Story of Esther	62
30	**Idol Nonsense**	Three Men in the Fiery Furnace	64
31	**Daily Witnessing**	Daniel in the Lion's Den	66
32	**Second Chances**	Jonah	68
33	**God's Timing**	The Birth of John Foretold	70
34	**Chosen**	The Birth of Jesus Foretold	72
35	**Sticks and Stones**	The Birth of John	74
36	**He's Got a Plan**	The Birth of Jesus	76
37	**The Young and the Faithful**	The Boy Jesus in the Temple	78
38	**New Beginnings**	The Baptism of Jesus	80
39	**Jesus: The Life of the Party?**	Jesus Changes Water into Wine	82
40	**Doing What Disciples Do**	Jesus Calls His Disciples	84
41	**Overcoming Adversity**	Jesus Heals a Man with Leprosy	86
42	**Forgiveness— The Greatest Miracle!**	Jesus Heals a Paralytic	88
43	**He's All That!**	Jesus Rejected at Nazareth	90
44	**Practical Parables**	Parables of Jesus	92
45	**One Thing Needed**	Mary and Martha	94
46	**Change-up**	The Transfiguration	96
47	**Building Up Your Strength**	The Lord's Supper	98
48	**The Most Amazing Story Ever Told**	Jesus' Death and Resurrection	100
49	**More Than Easter**	The Resurrection of Jesus	102
50	**No Doubt About It**	Jesus Appears to Thomas	104
51	**What's the Plan?**	The Ascension	106
52	**Pentecost Power**	God Sends the Holy Spirit	108

Introduction

Junior high students live in a confusing and increasingly complicated world. Their lives are often conflicted and torn as a result of sin. Sometimes it is sin from within, expressing itself in actions and attitudes that run counter to God's Law. Sometimes it is sin from other sources—the actions and attitudes of others—that disrupts their lives. They need God's help to live in the joy and fullness that Christ desires.

Since it is the Gospel that brings spiritual life in Christ to people, it is our goal in these Bible studies for junior high students to connect the Gospel to their life situations. These studies were prepared with four goals in mind. The lessons reflect these goals in the following ways:

1. Each lesson presents the Gospel in ways that will help young people grow in their relationship with Christ.

2. Each lesson is simple and direct—one page of instructions and helps for the Bible study leader and one reproducible page for the students to follow.

3. Each study is practical and easy to prepare. Interaction, variety, and active learning are stressed without requiring excessive preparation by the Bible study leader.

4. Each study deals with the Bible text and seeks to help young people apply the lesson to their lives as they seek to live in Christ.

This book contains fifty-two studies. They can be selected according to the needs of the students and leader and taught in any order.

HELPS FOR PREPARATION AND TEACHING

For ease of use, the leader page and student page for each study are printed side by side in this book, the leader's material on the left and the corresponding student page on the right. The appropriate student page should be copied in a quantity sufficient for the class and distributed at the time indicated in the leader's notes.

It is assumed that the Bible class leader will have the usual basic classroom equipment and supplies available—pencils or pens for each student, blank paper (and occasionally tape or marking pens), and a chalkboard or its equivalent (white board, overhead transparency projector, or newsprint pad and easel) with corresponding chalk or markers. Encourage the students to bring their own Bibles so that they can mark useful passages and make personal notes to guide their Bible study between classes. Do provide additional Bibles, however, for visitors or students who do not bring one.

The studies are outlined completely in the leader's notes, including a suggested time for each section of the study. The suggested times will total fifty to fifty-five minutes, the maximum amount most Sunday morning Bible classes have available. Each session begins with an opening activity that may or may not be indicated on the student page. Teachers who regularly begin with prayer should include it before the opening activity. Most other parts of the study, except the closing prayer, are on both the leader page and student page.

An average class size of ten students is assumed. To facilitate discussion, especially when your class is larger than average, it is recommended that you conduct much of the discussion in smaller breakout groups—pairs, triads, or groups of five or six. Instructions to that effect are often included in the guide. If your class is small, you are blessed to already have a "breakout group" and can ignore these suggestions. Leaders who prefer to do all discussion with the class as a whole are also free to ignore breakout-group suggestions.

Most of the studies include one or two "Lesson Extenders" suggestions. Use these when the study progresses more quickly than expected, when your normal session exceeds fifty to fifty-five minutes, or when a suggested activity doesn't work with your group. They can also be used as "during the week" activities.

Of course, the leader is encouraged to review the study thoroughly, well in advance of its presentation. That way the materials can be tailored to your individual students' needs and preferences as well as your own. A prepared and confident teacher normally has better classroom control, which results in a more positive experience for both students and leader.

1. Life Giving

Genesis 1:1–2:3

Lesson Focus

The creation account reminds us that God created the world simply by speaking. God has not left His creation alone, but continues to care for it today.

LIFE GIVING (10 minutes)

Have students brainstorm words or phrases that contain the word *life*. Record their suggestions on the board or newsprint. Ask students to define what each of their suggested words or phrases means. If students have not already suggested it, add the phrase "Life Giving" to the list. Discuss what this phrase means for us as believers in Christ. Remind students that God not only gives us physical life, but He gives and sustains our eternal life as well.

LIFE CREATING (20 minutes)

Distribute copies of Student Page 1. Three phrases occur repeatedly in Genesis 1:1–2:3: "God said/called"; "God saw that it was good"; "and it was so." List each of these phrases on the board or newsprint. Below each phrase, ask students to note the verses in which the phrase occurs. Help students identify the action or focus for each of these phrases. By His work of creating, God calls the world into existence, creating something out of nothing. That which He calls into being is good and perfect, as He intended it to be.

"Created in God's image" does not mean that humankind looks like God. Rather, Adam and Eve knew God and were holy and righteous, like Him. Humans lost that image at the fall into sin, and it remains incomplete to this day. Through Christ, God has begun to rebuild that image in believers, but only in heaven will it be fully restored (see Luther's Small Catechism, explanation of the First Article of the Apostles' Creed).

God blesses humans and wants them to multiply. God gives them responsibility to care for the earth. God declares His creation to be good.

LIFE SUSTAINING (15 minutes)

God did not leave His creation alone. Allow students to work alone or in pairs to review each of the verses and find the truths about God's continued care for His creation to this day. Review student findings as a whole group. Wrap up by emphasizing Hebrews 2:14–17. God has shown His greatest care for His creation by sending His only Son as the Savior from sin. Christ shared in humanity in order to save all who are created. Because He shared our humanity through His gift of faith, we receive atonement for our sins and share in His resurrection.

CLOSING (5 minutes)

Close with prayer, thanking God for His continued care of the world. Include any special prayer petitions that may have come up during the lesson today.

LESSON EXTENDERS

✝ Review the explanation of the First Article of the Apostles' Creed in Luther's Small Catechism.

✝ Study the text of "All Mankind Fell in Adam's Fall" (*LSB* 562, *LW* 363).

Life Giving

LIFE CREATING

Read **Genesis 1:1–2:3**. Three phrases occur frequently. What are they, and what do they mean?

Study **Genesis 1:26–27**. God has no form, yet humans are created in God's image. What does this mean?

See **Genesis 5:3** and **1 Corinthians 2:14**. What happened to our image of God?

Focus on **Genesis 1:28–31**. What words and images convey that God likes the humans He just created?

LIFE SUSTAINING

God did not leave His creation alone; He continues to care for us. What do each of these verses say about God's care for His creation?

Psalm 36:6

Psalm 103:13

Psalm 145:15–16

Matthew 10:28–31

Hebrews 2:14–17

1 Peter 5:7

2. A PRECIOUS GIFT

Genesis 2:4–25

Lesson Focus

God is the giver of all good things. Sexuality and relationships are among God's gifts—intended for our good, spoiled by sin, redeemed through Christ, and a model of His love for His people.

OPENING (10 minutes)

Prior to class, make two signs: on one write "Disposable," on the other write "Irreplaceable." Post the two signs on opposite sides of the classroom. Ask the students to move to either side of the room depending on how they view each of the items. Begin by mentioning items that are obviously disposable (such as paper diapers or alkaline batteries). Move to things that are irreplaceable (famous art or an engagement ring). Include interpersonal relationships (your best friend or your parents). Ask students to place the marriage relationship somewhere on the continuum. Discuss with students the idea that society often views things as disposable. That makes life convenient, but it can become detrimental when that attitude extends to relationships, especially marriage.

FOR ADAM AND EVE (15 minutes)

Distribute copies of Student Page 2. If your class is large, divide into small groups. Direct the students to Genesis 2:4–25. Ask each group to consider the questions found on the worksheet. Ask each group to appoint one leader who is to help the group reach a common response to the questions. When you sense that all groups are finished, ask the groups to share their responses. Remind students that God's purpose in uniting Adam and Eve was to provide companionship. His desire for Adam and Eve was a "one flesh," monogamous relationship of mutual respect and care—marriage.

FOR US (10 minutes)

Based on previous discussion, ask what God's desire is for teenagers when it comes to their sexuality. Allow the students to talk about the issue openly. Remind them that God's desire is that sexual intercourse is to be reserved for the marriage relationship. Direct the students to John 8:1–11, and ask a volunteer to read the passage aloud. Ask the participants to again discuss the questions on the student page in their small groups. God desires that all people honor the marriage relationship. He also stands ready to forgive all people, even those who commit the sin of adultery.

GOD'S GREATEST GIFT (15 minutes)

Ask a student to read aloud Ephesians 5:22–33. Again have students discuss the questions on the student page. Discuss with the class the amazing model for relationships given in these passages.

CLOSING (5 minutes)

Close with a group prayer. Ask students to pray specifically about relationships. Also thank God for His gift of sexuality and ask for His strength to use it in a way that is pleasing to Him.

LESSON EXTENDERS

✞ Have students brainstorm a list of television shows that depict couples and relationships. Discuss how these shows depict positive or negative values, based on what you've studied today.

✞ Invite a married couple to class to talk about their relationship. Focus on how they daily live out Paul's words in Ephesians 5.

A PRECIOUS GIFT

FOR ADAM AND EVE

Read **Genesis 2:4–25**.

What was God's purpose in uniting Adam and Eve?

....

What kind of relationship did God desire between Adam and Eve?

....

What role did God's gift of sexuality play in that relationship?

....

FOR US

Read **John 8:1–11**.

Of what sin was the woman accused?

....

What was Jesus' attitude toward the woman?

....

What message is Jesus sending to those who commit sins against the Sixth Commandment?

....

GOD'S GREATEST GIFT

Read **Ephesians 5:22–33**.

What model does Paul suggest to illustrate the love relationship of marriage?

....

Both for those who marry and those who remain single, what great Gospel message is in these verses concerning Christ and the Church?

....

Created in Christ © 2006 Concordia Publishing House. Reproduced by permission.

STUDENT PAGE 2

3. THE BLAME GAME

Genesis 3:1–24

Lesson Focus

Society often rationalizes sinful actions, blaming other people or things. In reality our sinful actions result from our sinful nature. The Good News is that Jesus has the cure for sin. He gives eternal life to all who believe in Him through the power of the Spirit.

OPENING (5 minutes)

Prior to the session, gather several newspaper articles containing examples of sin in society. As class begins, share these articles with the students and ask for their reactions. What other signs of sin do they see in the world? Have we become callous to sin, thinking of it as acceptable within our culture? Offer a brief prayer asking God's blessing on the session.

THREE SCENARIOS (10 minutes)

Distribute copies of Student Page 3. Read and discuss each of the three scenarios. How did the people try to rationalize their sinful actions? What other excuses do people use to justify actions that go against God's will? What negative effect does rationalizing our sinful action have on our relationship with God?

INTO THE WORD (15 minutes)

Like contemporary people, Adam and Eve tried to play the blame game. But God would not allow that. He lovingly sought them out and, in spite of the consequences, gave them a reason to hope. Direct the students to Genesis 3:1–24. Ask a volunteer to read the verses aloud. Divide the class into small groups to discuss the questions found on the student page. Remind the students that, while the serpent did tempt Eve, Adam and Eve decided to disobey God. In the same way, adults and teenagers need to assume responsibility for their bad decisions.

GOD'S LOVING RESPONSE (15 minutes)

Remind participants that God showed He still cared about Adam and Eve by promising them a Savior and also providing for their physical needs. Ask how God shows He cares for people today. Direct the students to Romans 5:12–21 and ask a volunteer to read it aloud. Ask how, according to Romans 5, sin came into the world. How did God's grace enter into the world? As baptized children of God, why do these verses give us reason to celebrate?

CLOSING (10 minutes)

Ask the students to follow along as you read Romans 6:1–7. Through Baptism, sin is put to death in our life and is replaced by new life in Christ. That renewal takes place on a daily basis as we come before God's throne of grace in confession and absolution. For the closing prayer, ask God to touch each member of the class on a daily basis, reminding them that they are His forgiven children.

LESSON EXTENDERS

✠ Have students create bookmarks using verses from Romans 5. Cover them with clear adhesive paper. Have students use this in books they see daily as a reminder of God's daily grace to us.

THE BLAME GAME

THREE SCENARIOS

Theo was an above-average student in chemistry, but he always seemed to do poorly on tests. He was frustrated because he knew some of his classmates often cheated to get better grades. When his friends approached him with a stolen copy of an upcoming test, Theo jumped at the chance to improve his grade. Theo didn't realize that the teacher had planted the test, hoping to catch dishonest students. When confronted, Theo explained, "Everyone cheats. I was just trying to get the grade I deserve."

Connie often spent Saturday afternoon at the mall with her friends. One Saturday her friend Shelly suggested that they shoplift some cosmetics from a department store. Her other friend, Wendy, quickly agreed. When Connie objected, the girls made fun of her. Connie eventually gave in because she was afraid of losing her friends. The girls got caught, and the store turned the girls over to their parents. When her mother confronted her, Connie said, "It was Shelly and Wendy's idea. They made me to do it."

Conrad's parents divorced when he was very young. With his mother working long hours, Conrad had a lot of free time. His mother was always tired when she was home and his dad, an alcoholic, didn't care. In middle school Conrad started hanging out with a "bad" crowd. In high school he and several of his friends were arrested for destructive vandalism. When questioned, Conrad was quick to point out that he would never amount to anything because he came from a lousy home.

INTO THE WORD

Read **Genesis 3:1–24**.

What motivated Eve and Adam to eat the forbidden fruit?

What role did the serpent play?

What were the consequences of Eve and Adam's decision?

How does their decision affect us today?

GOD'S LOVING RESPONSE

Read **Romans 5:12–21**. What Good News does Paul remind us of, even though we are sinful?

Created in Christ © 2006 Concordia Publishing House. Reproduced by permission.

4. GOD'S ATTITUDE

Genesis 4:1–16; Romans 2:4

Lesson Focus

Our attitude toward God's gifts to us often reflects our sinful nature. Yet God demonstrates His never-failing love, grace, and forgiveness as He chooses and marks us as His own.

OPENING (5 minutes)

Ask students to prepare a list of the gifts God has given them and how they use those gifts in service to God. Remind students to consider not only material gifts, but talents and spiritual blessings as well. Record their list on the board or newsprint.

GIFTS FROM ABOVE (10 minutes)

Distribute copies of Student Page 4. Have the students read Genesis 4:1–2. When discussing these verses, help students see that God gave Abel and Cain the responsibility to shepherd the flocks and work the fields. These were the vocations God had given. Their vocations were equally important. The issue in this story comes in the attitudes with which Abel and Cain gave their offerings to God.

ATTITUDES FROM BELOW (20 minutes)

Discuss the opening question as a whole group. Ask for a volunteer to read Genesis 4:3–14. In breakout groups, have the students compile an outline of this section of Scripture. In the whole group, combine the outlines and use the result as a guide throughout the remainder of the class. As you discuss Hebrews 11:4 and the remaining questions of this section, be sure students understand that the difference in Abel's and Cain's offerings was not in the gifts, but in the attitude with which they were given. Hebrews 11:4 says Abel brought his gift in faith, thereby making his offering better than Cain's in the eyes of the Lord. Because of Cain's attitude God did not look upon his offering with favor. God's reaction led Cain to become angry and ultimately to kill his brother, thereby compounding the negative results of his poor attitude.

MARKS FROM ABOVE (10 minutes)

As you wrap up this discussion, help students to see the progression of the consequences of Cain's first mistake of presenting his offering with a poor attitude. His contempt for the gifts God had given him led to additional sins. According to Genesis 4:15–16, God still provided protection for Cain. Read Romans 2:4. Despite the numerous sins we commit and our selfish attitudes, God promises to always love and protect us. Romans 5:1–2 reminds us that our salvation is secured because of Christ. Help students understand that it is the love of Christ that leads us to repent and give joyfully of the gifts God has given us. Discuss ways in which students can use their God-given gifts in response to His love and forgiveness.

CLOSING (5 minutes)

Close by inviting students to pray in turn, thanking God for one of the gifts they listed in the opening activity.

LESSON EXTENDERS

✝ Develop plans for a church or community servant event using some of the gifts the students listed in the opening activity. Have each student write a letter to God, giving thanks for being chosen as His child and for being blessed with His gifts.

GOD'S ATTITUDE

GIFTS FROM ABOVE

Read **Genesis 4:1–2**. As God gives us gifts, He also gives us responsibility.

What gift and corresponding responsibility did God give Abel? Cain?

Is one of these gifts or responsibilities of greater value than the other? Why or why not?

ATTITUDES FROM BELOW

When someone gives you a gift, what is your normal reaction?

Read **Genesis 4:3–14**. Outline what happened, paying close attention to Cain's and Abel's offerings. What is the difference between how God looks upon the offerings?

Read **Hebrews 11:4**. Why does God look with favor upon Abel and his offering?

What do you think Cain's attitude was when he brought his offering to God?

What happens within the family as a result of Cain's poor attitude?

MARKS FROM ABOVE

In **Genesis 4:14** Cain worried that he would be killed as he wandered upon the earth as a consequence of killing his brother. Read **Genesis 4:15–16**. What is God's response to Cain's worry?

Read **Romans 2:4**. Sometimes we, like Cain, show contempt toward God and the gifts He gives us. Yet God continues to love us and leads us toward repentance. Read **Romans 5:1–2**. Just as God forgave Cain and placed a mark on him, He has forgiven us and placed His mark on us in our Baptism. As a result of God's great love for us, how can we respond to Him?

5. BY FAITH

Genesis 6:1–9:17

Lesson Focus

Christian young people are eager to know God's will for their lives. Today's lesson will focus on how we live by faith in the grace of God.

OPENING (10 minutes)

Ask students to share a time they have been asked to do something that didn't make sense. What was it? Who asked them to do it? If they were one of Noah's sons, would they have remained faithful to the project God placed before Dad, or would they have left because they thought he was crazy or because of the taunting of the people around them?

THE REMARKABLE ARK (15 minutes)

Distribute copies of Student Page 5. Most students will be familiar with the story of Noah and the flood. Introduce the story by reading Genesis 6:11–7:5. Have students work together to answer the questions from the student page. Discuss their answers.

(The ark was about one and two-thirds football fields long, one full-sized basketball court wide, and five and a half stories high. Noah took more of the clean animals because he needed to have animals for food and for an offering to God. The clean animals were those acceptable for eating under Jewish dietary laws. The unclean animals were needed to repopulate the earth. Noah lived in a desert region without many trees. There were no cranes or power tools for assembling the ark. Noah did everything as God had commanded.)

GET ON BOARD (10 minutes)

Have the students read 2 Peter 2:5. Allow the students to work together to answer the questions from the student page. (In the time leading up to the flood, Noah was busy preparing the ark, loading supplies and animals, and worshiping God. Life on the ark was probably kept busy with the activities of daily living, plus caring for their cargo. Given the lack of many windows and the rain, it was probably fairly dark inside the ark.)

RAINBOW REMEMBRANCES (10 minutes)

Have students read the verses from the student page and discuss their findings.

Review God's promise to Noah and his family in Genesis 8:21–22 and Genesis 9:8–17. What promises does God make to His people? (God promised to never again curse the ground and never to destroy the earth with a flood again. As a further sign of His promise and covenant with mankind, God used the rainbow as a reminder that He would never again destroy the earth with a flood.)

CLOSING (5 MINUTES)

Close in prayer, thanking God for the Old Testament faithful and the example they set for us. Thank God for sending His Son to complete the work of salvation for us.

LESSON EXTENDERS

✝ Have groups create a skit of a television news team interviewing the "crew" of the ark after they have made a sacrifice to the Lord. The skit could be presented to the class.

✝ Read together Hebrews 11:1–40. Create a "Faith's Hall of Fame." Teams of students could write citations (and create plaques) for each "hero of faith."

BY FAITH

THE REMARKABLE ARK

Read **Genesis 6:11–7:5**.

Given the dimensions of the ark, what could you compare it to?

....

....

What details of the ark surprise you?

....

....

Why do you think Noah was supposed to take only one pair of the unclean animals and seven pairs of the clean animals?

....

....

What difficulties do you suppose Noah faced in building the ark?

....

....

What words remind us of Noah's acceptance of God's direction?

....

....

....

GET ON BOARD

Read **2 Peter 2:5**.

What might Noah have been doing up until the time God closed the door to the ark?

....

Based on what you've read, what was life on the ark like?

....

....

RAINBOW REMEMBRANCES

Noah was rescued through God's grace from a world drowning in sin, floating through the flood in the ark. What does God promise His people about His future treatment of sinful people? (See **Genesis 8:21–22** and **9:8–17**.)

....

....

How did God fulfill that covenant promise? (See **1 Peter 3:18–21**.)

....

....

Read **Hebrews 11:7, 39–40**. What really saved Noah? What does God have in mind for you?

....

....

Created in Christ © 2006 Concordia Publishing House. Reproduced by permission.

6. Saved by Faith!

Genesis 12:1–9

Lesson Focus

We rejoice that, through faith in Jesus Christ, God has made us heirs of eternal life and children of Abraham, the father of the faithful!

EVER MOVED?
(10 minutes)

Distribute copies of Student Page 6 and ask students to respond to the question concerning their fear of moving. List the top three fears on the board. Fears may include leaving friends; a strange school; loneliness; having to rethink high school plans; and so forth. Say: "The point is that moving is frightening—no matter at what age! Today we see how Abraham was told by God to move to an unfamiliar country and what blessings would be his if he would trust the Lord."

A SHOW OF FAITH
(20 minutes)

Invite students to answer the three questions.

Faith does *not* rely on visible proof, but trusts the Word of God because God said it (see Hebrews 11:1). Jesus said: "You did not choose Me, but *I chose you* and appointed you to go and bear fruit—fruit that will last" (John 15:16, emphasis added). Obedience is the "fruit" of faith. Faith *alone* in Jesus saves us. Where there is faith, the Holy Spirit also has given us the desire to please God with cheerful obedience to Him.

Students may work together in breakout groups to read the Bible passages and discuss the questions. Review their answers.

God promised Abraham that "all peoples on earth will be blessed through you" (Genesis 12:3). God was talking about *us*! That blessing was the Savior of the world—Jesus. All who trust in Christ are children of Abraham who believed God's promises!

Abraham proved he trusted God by taking his wife, Sarah, and all they had and moving!

God first speaks to us in His Word, and we respond in prayer, praise, and thanksgiving.

God spoke directly to Abraham. God speaks to us today through His Word, Baptism, and the Lord's Supper. Our faith in Jesus is nourished every time we worship God.

Since Abraham trusted the Lord, he knew that God would never lie to him. He looked forward to the day God's Savior would appear (see John 8:56–58).

ABRAHAM'S CHILDREN THROUGH FAITH
(15 minutes)

Read the paragraph and question. Say, "Being a child of Abraham through faith in Jesus means we are God's children! Our sins are removed from us 'as far as the east is from the west' (Psalm 103:12). When we or someone we know is frightened, God bids us to trust Him as did Abraham."

CLOSING (5 minutes)

Invite students to mention those who are in special need. Then let them pray individually, in pairs, or in groups using this model: "Lord Jesus, we trust in You to save us. Please help _____ with the comfort and strength only You can give. In Your name we pray. Amen."

Saved by Faith!

EVER MOVED?
Name three things you would fear if you had to move right now.

....

....

....

A SHOW OF FAITH
Does faith rely upon visible proof?

....

Do we choose to follow God?

....

What is the connection between faith and obedience?

....

Read **Genesis 12:1–3**. How can we be called "children of Abraham"?

....

Read **Genesis 12:4–5**. How did Abraham prove that he trusted God?

....

Read **Genesis 12:6–7**. In worship, who speaks to whom first?

....

Read **Genesis 12:8–9**. What is the connection between faith and worship?

....

Read **Hebrews 11:8–10**. Why was Abraham willing to leave his homeland and go to the land God told him?

....

ABRAHAM'S CHILDREN THROUGH FAITH!

Abraham obeyed God's call and took his wife, Sarah, to the Promised Land. This land eventually became the land of Israel—the "great nation" God promised to Abraham. Though many were *unfaithful* throughout Israel's Old Testament history, God remained faithful and kept His promise to send the Savior of the world! Through Jesus' death on the cross and resurrection, "all peoples on earth" **(Genesis 12:3)** were blessed through this one perfect Son of Abraham. All of us who believe and are baptized into Christ are true children of Abraham—the father of the faithful!

When a friend goes through frightening events, how can we use Abraham's faithful example to encourage him or her?

....

....

....

....

Created in Christ © 2006 Concordia Publishing House. Reproduced by permission.

7. Do You Trust Me?

Genesis 22:1–19

Lesson Focus

God did not hold anything back when He gave Christ to be our Savior. Through faith in Christ, God empowers us to trust Him for all things

DO YOU REALLY TRUST ME? (10 minutes)

Have students pair up with someone of similar body size. Students will perform a "trust fall" by falling backward and being caught by their partner. The falling partner keeps legs straight as he or she falls straight backward. The faller does not go far at all, just enough to feel a desire to step backward. Use a verbal check system to make sure that pairs are ready. (For example: "Ready to fall?" "Falling." "Fall away.") Practice and demonstrate for students with a trusted adult.

After both partners have had the opportunity to fall, discuss the following: How did it feel to fall? (Unsettling, made them nervous) How did it feel to catch? (Reassuring, sense of control) Whom do you trust the most in your life? (Answers will vary, perhaps a parent or close friend) How does that trust get tested in your relationship with that person? (Answers will vary.)

DIGGING IN (15 minutes)

Read together Genesis 22:1–19. Distribute copies of Student Page 7. Allow students time to complete the questions from this section and discuss as a whole group. Students may be surprised that God tested Abraham like this or that Abraham followed God's instructions. Abraham may have questioned why, after waiting for a son, God wanted Abraham to kill Isaac. Isaac probably wondered what was happening, or perhaps he was trusting God. God used this testing to demonstrate Abraham's faith. Abraham knew God gave him Isaac in the first place; through faith he trusted God.

DIGGING DEEPER (15 minutes)

Have students work together in breakout groups to answer the questions from this section. After allowing time for students to discuss, call them together to share their insights. Through the lineage of Abraham and Isaac, God would provide a Savior. Both Abraham and God were willing to sacrifice their only sons. God gave us Jesus as the very sacrifice for sin that He demanded.

TAKING IT HOME (10 minutes)

Wrap up with asking for responses to each of the areas listed. Discuss each statement. Help students understand that, since we are both saint and sinner, it is impossible for us to trust completely. Emphasize that we can rely on God for the work of our salvation because of what Jesus Christ did for us. We cannot put ourselves in the equation of salvation. We know that it is completely a work of God, not our own. God forgives our weaknesses and restores us even when we fail to trust Him completely.

CLOSING (2 minutes)

Close with prayer: "Heavenly Father, You are truly a loving Father who has given us more than we deserve. We know that we don't trust You like we should with our lives. We often fail to see the great plans You have in store for us. Forgive our lack of faith in You and empower us with Your Spirit to trust completely in You, our loving Father. In Your Son's name we pray. Amen."

DO YOU TRUST ME?

DIGGING IN

Read together **Genesis 22:1–19**. What is the most surprising part of this Bible passage to you?

What do you think was most surprising to Abraham?

What do you think Isaac was thinking?

What do you think God was trying to demonstrate?

What made Abraham willing to give up his son?

How do **Hebrews 11:17–19** and **Genesis 22:5** shed light on Abraham's trust in God?

DIGGING DEEPER

How are Abraham and Isaac involved in God's plan of salvation (see **Matthew 1:1–2**)?

What parallels are there between what Abraham was asked to do and what God did?

Abraham said, "God Himself will provide the lamb" (**Genesis 22:8**). How is this true for us (see **John 1:29**)?

TAKING IT HOME

How can we rely on God concerning each of these aspects of our lives?

Future plans

Choosing friends

Money

Salvation

Created in Christ © 2006 Concordia Publishing House. Reproduced by permission.

8. Telling His Story

Genesis 24:1–67

Lesson Focus

This lesson encourages young people in their faith and helps them tell their personal stories of God's loving actions in their lives.

OPENING (5 minutes)

As students arrive, begin generating a list of the "Top Five Things Junior High Students Like to Do." Post the completed list to be used later.

TELLING YOUR STORY (15 minutes)

Distribute copies of Student Page 8. We all share many common experiences in life, but what makes them special is what happened to *you*! Let the students tell their stories. Have students work in pairs. Give directions and allow time for sharing.

1. Ask each student to choose one item from the "Top Five" list and share briefly about the best time they had doing that activity. Allow one minute for one student to share, then reverse roles and let the other person share for one minute.
2. Ask each student to choose one item from the "Telling Your Story" section of the student page. They should share briefly about the first time they ever did that activity. Give each student one minute to share.
3. Ask each student to share briefly about something God did in their life this past week. Again, allow one minute for each person.

Say, "Why can it be harder to talk about what God is doing than about what we like to do? Telling about school activities and life events can often be easier than telling about God's actions. Today we'll see that God's actions give us a story to tell."

WITH EYES WIDE OPEN (15 MINUTES)

Read aloud the opening paragraph of this section on the student page. Then read each portion of Genesis 24 and discuss the questions as a class. Ask the students, "If you had been Abraham's servant, would you have had faith in God? Why?"

Invite students to look briefly at a New Testament story from Acts 4. Read together verses 1–3 and ask what message the disciples proclaimed. Why were they jailed?

Read verse 20 and discuss the disciples' explanation for their actions.

Read verse 33. Even after they had been arrested and jailed, what did the disciples persist in doing?

God acted in our lives through the suffering, death, and resurrection of Jesus Christ. By the power of the Holy Spirit, He continues to act today so we can tell His story.

DO YOU SEE HIM? (15 minutes)

Encourage students to share God's actions in their lives and to practice telling His story. Remind students that God uses His Word and Sacraments as means of grace—specific ways in which He intersects with our lives through His Spirit. Prayer is our means of communicating our needs to Him. Our family and others provide the community in which faith is taught. God's power and faithfulness are on display within nature. Encourage the students to choose one or more of the "story starters," make some notes about how God is active in their life, and share their story with a partner.

CLOSING (5 minutes)

Close by reading Psalm 146 responsively by whole verse.

LESSON EXTENDERS

✞ Have students write an essay on God's actions in their lives. Share the essays in future class sessions.

✞ Encourage students to "tell their story" this week to someone who is not a Christian. Ask them to report back next week.

TELLING HIS STORY

TELLING YOUR STORY

Let me tell you about the first time I . . .
cooked a meal   scrubbed a toilet
acted in a drama   did the wash
changed a diaper   played in a concert
broke a bone   drove a car

WITH EYES WIDE OPEN

As Abraham's life drew to a close, he directed his chief servant, probably a man named Eliezer, to find a bride for his son Isaac. This bride would not be from among local pagans, but from among Abraham's relatives in Mesopotamia. Abraham's faith in God was certain. Check out the story of his success.

Read **Genesis 24:7–9**. Abraham had faith! Did his servant?

Read **Genesis 24:10–14**. Whose help did the servant seek? What did he ask for?

Read **Genesis 24:15–21**. Who was Rebekah? Was all of this pure luck? Why?

Read **Genesis 24:22–27**. Why did the servant bow down and worship God on the spot?

Abraham's servant recognized God's action in his life. He responded in worship and in what other way? (See **verses 33, 48**, and **50–51**.)

Scan the events of **Acts 4**. Look for similarities to **Genesis 24**.

DO YOU SEE HIM?

Abraham's servant saw God act in a search for a bride. The apostles saw Him alive from the tomb. They all had a story they told over and over to all who were near. Tell some of the stories of God's actions in your life. How does God act for you . . .

in your Baptism and in Holy Communion?

through Bible study?

in response to prayer?

through your family and others?

within nature?

Created in Christ © 2006 Concordia Publishing House. Reproduced by permission.

9. GOD'S BLESSINGS

Genesis 25:19–34; 27:1–29

Lesson Focus

We don't deserve God's blessings, but through His divine grace and mercy He blesses us abundantly.

OPENING (10 minutes)

Have students play a quick game (tic-tac-toe, spoons, a video game, or something similar), and reward the losers of the game with a special treat. Gather the group together, and ask students to respond to the following:

What do you think about our opening game and rewards? (It was backward, confusing, fun to lose.) How did it feel to win? to lose? (Answers will vary.) Have you ever been rewarded before without deserving it? When? (Answers will vary.) How did it make you feel? (Grateful, humble, not sure why they were being rewarded)

DIGGING IN (15 minutes)

Read Genesis 25:19–34; 27:1–29. If time allows, have volunteers act out the story. Distribute copies of Student Page 9. Allow students to work in breakout groups to answer the questions from this section. Discuss their answers with the whole group. The birthright was extremely important in biblical times, yet Esau was willing to give it up for some food. His attitude toward the birthright perhaps reflects his lack of understanding or immaturity. His attitude may reflect how we sometimes treat the blessings that God gives to us. Jacob plotted together with Rebekah to get Esau's blessing. Though he may have been undeserving, Jacob received his father's blessing.

DIGGING DEEPER (10 minutes)

Jacob and Esau parallel the nation of Israel and its rejection of God over and over. The Jews were God's chosen people, but they finally rejected their Savior, Jesus. Help students make this connection, and encourage them to go back to the story and find possible analogies to our relationship to God. Esau rejected his birthright over a physical need. Israel was God's "firstborn," but most Jews rejected God's blessings. Gentiles were welcomed into God's family and received God's blessing. Both brothers are undeserving of love, but God loves all because of His grace.

TAKING IT HOME (10 minutes)

Discuss the questions from this section with the whole group. We reject God's blessings by not following His will and by making our own choices. Our "birthright" is made secure at the cross and sealed at our Baptism into faith. We look to God to direct our lives. Finally, we receive the full measure of blessings in heaven. God's grace and love are undeserved but freely given.

CLOSING (5 minutes)

Say, "It may seem unfair to us how God chose to love Jacob. When we look at ourselves and others, we see that everyone is undeserving of God's love. Yet God has shown His mercy on the unlovable and undeserving, including us."

Close with prayer: "Loving Father, You have made us Your children in our Baptism and called us Your very own. Forgive us for not always remembering that we are members of Your family and for not acting as Your children. We thank You for the many blessings You give to us now and the blessings awaiting us in heaven. Help us to see with eyes focused on You. In Jesus' name we pray. Amen."

GOD'S BLESSINGS

DIGGING IN

Read **Genesis 25:19–34** and **27:1–29**. Why did Esau give up his birthright?

The birthright was extremely important in biblical times, yet Esau gave it away readily. What might this reflect concerning his attitude toward the birthright?

....

....

Who was the most at fault in this story for Esau losing his blessing—Esau, Isaac, Jacob, or Rebekah? Why?

....

....

How do you feel knowing that the undeserving son got the blessing?

....

....

DIGGING DEEPER

Jacob and Esau parallel Israel and its rejection of God over and over. The Jews were God's chosen people, but they finally rejected their Savior, Jesus. Go back through the story and find analogies concerning God's relationship with humankind.

....

....

....

....

TAKING IT HOME

In what ways have you rejected God's blessings? (**John 3:36**; **1 Peter 2:7–8**)

....

....

How has God made secure our "birthright"? (**2 Corinthians 1:20–22**)

....

....

How can we enjoy the benefits of God's blessings? (**Romans 6:21–23**)

....

....

How is God's plan at work in this story and in your story?

....

....

Created in Christ © 2006 Concordia Publishing House. Reproduced by permission.

10. Bad That Works For Good

Genesis 37:1–36; 39:1–41:57

Lesson Focus

Joseph's life experiences remind believers that God is with them even during bad events in their lives.

OPENING (5 minutes)

Distribute copies of Student Page 10. Ask students to read the opening quote and discuss what they believe Luther meant. Ask for volunteers to share about a time in their lives when they thought what was happening was bad, but it ended up being good.

BAD THINGS DO HAPPEN TO GOOD PEOPLE (15 minutes)

Divide students into four breakout groups, and assign selected verses to each group. Direct students to read the assigned verses, summarize the event, and share their discoveries with the whole group. Events: Joseph was stripped and thrown into a cistern; Joseph was sold into slavery (he was seventeen); Potiphar's wife lied about Joseph and he was imprisoned; and the cupbearer forgot about Joseph (which meant he remained in prison). Ask students to consider how Joseph may have felt as these events took place. What might he have been thinking? What were his prayers? What are some of the typical human responses to these types of events happening in one's life?

GOD WORKS FOR THE GOOD OF THOSE WHO LOVE HIM (10 minutes)

Ask two volunteers to read Genesis 39:1–6 and 39:20–23 aloud; point others to directions on the student page. Discuss together the findings. These include how the Lord *was with* Joseph, the Lord *gave* Joseph success in everything he did, and God *showed* Joseph kindness and *granted* him favor in the eyes of the prison warden.

GOD PRESERVES JOSEPH'S FAITH (10 minutes)

Have everyone turn to Ephesians 6:7–8 and read the passage aloud together. Return to breakout groups, assigning one passage to each group. Ask each group to share how they see Ephesians 6:7–8 fulfilled in the way Joseph went about his work as a slave and a prisoner. Responses: Joseph refused to sin against God and Potiphar by committing adultery; Joseph gives the glory to God for interpreting dreams, rather than to himself; Potiphar had no worries, because Joseph was in charge; Joseph was a hard worker—he collected, stored, and kept record of the food.

GOD PRESERVES ME (10 minutes)

Ask students to prayerfully consider their responses to bad events in their lives and to read the Romans passage on their own. Tell them that answers do not need to be shared, but that you will ask if anyone is willing to do so. Allow three to five minutes for students to read the passage. Ask for volunteers to share. Close with prayer, thanking God that He "works for the good of those who love Him" (Romans 8:28).

LESSON EXTENDERS

✝ Look up the five dreams in this lesson (Genesis 37:5–7; 37:9; 40:9–13; 40:16–18; 41:1–32). Discuss the dreams in the light of this quote by Luther regarding dreams: "How are we to distinguish between dreams from God or from Satan? The Holy Spirit not only sends dreams, but explains them and fulfills them. For myself I desire neither visions nor dreams, for it is sufficient for me that I have the sacred Scriptures which fully teach me all things necessary both in this life and that to come."

Bad That Works For Good

BAD THINGS DO HAPPEN TO GOOD PEOPLE

Read the following passages and summarize the bad events that took place in Joseph's life.

Genesis 37:23–24

Genesis 37:28 (Also read **37:2** and note how old Joseph was when these events took place.)

Genesis 39:6–20

Genesis 40:14–15, 23

GOD WORKS FOR THE GOOD OF THOSE WHO LOVE HIM

Write down words in the following two passages that describe where God was and what God was doing during the low points of Joseph's life.

Genesis 39:1–6

GOD PRESERVES JOSEPH'S FAITH

Consider how Joseph lived out **Ephesians 6:7–8** as you read the following passages

Genesis 39:6

Genesis 39:8–10

Genesis 41:15–16, 25

Genesis 41:46–49

> It is disagreeable to the flesh to be led in another way than the one reason argues one should be led. But it is the only safe way to be led by God.
>
> — *Martin Luther*

GOD PRESERVES ME

When bad things happen to you, are you more likely to pray . . .

> God, where are You?
> Why are You doing this to me?
>
> or
>
> I don't understand, but I know You are in control. I trust You.

How could **Romans 8:28** and **Romans 8:37–39** provide comfort in times of difficulty?

STUDENT PAGE 10

Created in Christ © 2006 Concordia Publishing House. Reproduced by permission.

11. Heart Check

Genesis 42:1–45:28; 50:15–21

Lesson Focus

Many young people carry a burden of guilt, while others feel no regret for their sins. In this lesson, students learn how God helps us repent of our sin and then move beyond it as we trust Jesus to forgive us and help us live for Him.

IT'S JUST A TEST (10 minutes)

Prepare samples of a popular brand and a generic brand of cola, peanut butter, or another product. Challenge students to identify the generic brand by looks alone. How can you test these products to find the differences? Allow students to sample the products and note the differences that can be found through a taste test. Discuss the questions on the student page.

BRUISED BY SIN (15 minutes)

Distribute copies of Student Page 11. Have students read through the Bible references and answer the questions. Emphasize that Joseph may not have challenged his brothers out of revenge. He may have been testing them to see if they had repented of their sin or if they were the same hardhearted brothers who had ignored his cries and sold him into slavery years before.

HEALED BY FORGIVENESS (15 minutes)

Read and discuss the Bible references. Say, "What evidence do you see that Joseph still loves his brothers? How does forgiving someone who has not repented show love? Joseph knew God's forgiving love. Since he loved his brothers, he wanted them to know God's forgiveness too. If Joseph's brothers were not sorry and did not repent of their sin, they would not know God's forgiveness. Joseph lovingly did what he could to create a loving and forgiving relationship."

MY SIN AND GOD'S SOLUTION (10 minutes)

After you read the verses about sin, allow time for students to reflect on the sin in their own hearts. Work through the remaining verses, emphasizing the words of God's forgiveness. Speak of the comfort God brings to each believer through faith in Jesus. Ask, "How does Satan use guilt to draw us away from God? Satan wins when we reject God's forgiveness and continue in our sin. God wants us to live joyfully, trusting Him to supply the grace to cover even our worst sins, as He helps us look forward to living in heaven with Him."

CLOSING (5 minutes)

Ask students to skim Psalm 103 and identify phrases that assure them they are forgiven. If time is short, concentrate on verses 1–12. Close by reading the psalm, alternating by whole verse.

LESSON EXTENDERS

✝ Discuss: Should a prisoner's lack of remorse for her crime be taken into account when she is being sentenced or considered for parole? When are feelings of guilt good? When are they harmful? For help see Psalm 32:3–5 and 1 John 1:8–10.

✝ Study together the Confession and Absolution portion of the liturgy (*LSB*, p. 167; *LW*, pp. 158–159). Ask, "Why is this part of the service so important? What feelings does it bring? Why?"

Heart Check

IT'S JUST A TEST

What can you learn by taking a test? What can you learn by giving one?

....

Why are tests so important at school? the hospital? factories?

....

BRUISED BY SIN

Joseph had been sold as a slave by his brothers. Most people would have thoughts of revenge or concerns for other members of the family. Why might each of these questions have gone through Joseph's mind? What do you think the answers might be?

Are my brothers tormenting Benjamin now?

....

Are they burdened with guilt?

....

Have they forgotten what they did to me?

....

How is my father?

....

How will my life end up?

....

What test did Joseph give his brothers? (**Genesis 42:6–20**)

....

What was their response? (**Genesis 42:21–28**)

....

During the brothers' second visit to Egypt, Joseph wanted to observe their relationship with Benjamin. He tested them again.

What were the tests? (**Genesis 4:34–44:17**)

....

What did Joseph learn about his brothers? (**Genesis 44:18–34**)

....

HEALED BY FORGIVENESS

What did Joseph do when he saw his brothers' repentant hearts? (**Genesis 45:1–15**)

....

After their father died, the brothers were afraid Joseph would try to get revenge. They still had guilty hearts. How does Joseph reassure them? (**Genesis 50:15–21**)

....

Do you think Joseph would have forgiven his brothers if they were not sorry for what they had done? How does God create repentant hearts? How does that prepare us for the forgiveness He offers?

....

MY SIN AND GOD'S SOLUTION

What does God's Word teach us about our sin? (**James 4:17; 1 John 1:8**)

....

What does it teach us about forgiveness? (**1 John 1:9**)

....

Satan may tempt us to doubt God's forgiving love and wallow in our guilt. How do the following verses reassure us? (**Ephesians 2:4–5; 1 John 4:9–10**)

....

Created in Christ © 2006 Concordia Publishing House. Reproduced by permission.

12. GOD'S CALLING

Exodus 2–4

Lesson Focus

Through the redeeming work of Christ, God calls us in Holy Baptism to be His children and sends us to share His love with others.

THE CALLING (5 minutes)

Distribute copies of Student Page 12. Engage students in a discussion about the word *calling*. A calling can also be called a *vocation*, a job or the course of a person's life. Ask how students would define their callings, suggesting ideas such as student, daughter/son, nephew/niece, brother/sister, worker, and so forth. Encourage them to give examples of those who forsake their callings—mothers who have abortions; kids who rebel against their parents; students who ignore their schoolwork. Transition into a discussion about Moses and his calling.

GOD CALLS MOSES (15 minutes)

Briefly review the dramatic story of Moses' birth (Exodus 2:1–4), his adoption by Pharaoh's daughter (Exodus 2:5–10), his murder of the Egyptian guard (Exodus 2:11–14), and his flight to Midian (Exodus 2:15–25). God showed His kindness to Moses by sustaining him through many difficulties.

As students look up the verses in Exodus and answer the questions, encourage them to notice how the Lord responds to Moses' lack of confidence when he is asked to perform these important tasks for God's people. God is patient and reassuring, but Moses keeps doubting. Finally, God suggests that Moses bring along his brother to help.

GOD CALLS ME (20 minutes)

Have students read 2 Thessalonians 2:13–14 in pairs and answer the question. God calls through the Gospel. Review with students the meaning of this familiar word—the Good News about Jesus dying for us and rising again to forgive our sins.

Next, have students look up Titus 3:5–7, pointing them to Baptism as a means of grace. God grants us faith through Baptism and gives us hope for eternal life through the sacrifice and love of our Savior, Jesus.

CALLING OTHERS (5 minutes)

God's grace for sinners, given to us through Christ's sacrifice and applied to us in Baptism, is wonderful news to share with others. Like Moses, we have God's reassurance that He is with us as we fulfill our callings in the world, sharing His love with others as we live out our vocations.

The 2 Thessalonians passage could be summarized this way: *stand firm* (2:15–17); *pray* (3:1–3); and *trust in the Lord* (3:4–5).

CLOSING (5 minutes)

Consider closing with "Listen, God Is Calling" (*LSB* 833, *HS98* 872) or another hymn celebrating God's kindness to us and sharing that Good News with others. Pray, "Our Father, we thank You for calling us through the Good News of salvation in Jesus, applying that Good News to us in Baptism, and reassuring us as we share that Good News with others. In Christ's name we pray. Amen."

LESSON EXTENDERS

✝ Review the Third Article of the Apostles' Creed from Luther's Small Catechism. Encourage students to note that all three persons of the Trinity are mentioned in 2 Thessalonians 2:13–14. Discuss the importance of the work of the Holy Spirit, as well as of the Father and the Son.

GOD'S CALLING

THE CALLING

What is a calling? What are some of your callings (son/daughter, student, etc.)?

....

....

What happens if callings, or vocations, are ignored?

....

....

GOD CALLS MOSES

Through Moses' dramatic birth, adoption by Pharaoh's daughter, murder of the Egyptian guard, and flight to Midian, how did God show His kindness to Moses?

....

....

Read **Exodus 3:1–10**. What was the mission God sent Moses to accomplish?

....

....

What was Moses' response to God's plea? (See **Exodus 3:11; 4:1, 10, 13**.)

....

....

How did God reassure him? (See **Exodus 3:12; 4:2–9, 11–12**.)

....

What was God's final solution? (See **Exodus 4:14–17**.)

....

....

GOD CALLS ME

Read **2 Thessalonians 2:13–14**. From these verses, how did God call you?

....

Read **Titus 3:5–7**. What is the means God uses to save us? What is our hope?

....

....

What did Jesus do to bring about the blessings of Baptism and salvation?

....

How does this relate to your calling?

....

CALLING OTHERS

What is the Good News we can share with others?

....

How can we be encouraged to share this Good News with others, as Moses did?

....

Read **2 Thessalonians 2:15–3:5**. What three phrases would you use to describe St. Paul's advice to the Thessalonians?

....

STUDENT PAGE 12

13. GOD PASSES OVER

Exodus 12:1–30

Lesson Focus

Just as God spared the Israelites in the Passover, so He spares us because of Christ's sacrifice for sin in order to redeem us.

OPENING (5 minutes)

Begin a discussion about guilt and responsibility. Have students recall a time when they were punished for someone else's wrongdoing (a sister disciplined for something her brother did, etc.). Ask students to describe that kind of punishment. "It's not fair" is the tried-and-true refrain demanding justice.

EGYPT'S SIN (15 minutes)

Distribute copies of Student Page 13. Continue the discussion with students about guilt and punishment by moving to the subject of Exodus 12. Briefly review the preceding Exodus passages about God's demand that Pharaoh release the Israelites from slavery. Emphasize the stubbornness of Pharaoh in refusing to submit to God's demands. This sets the stage for the final "sign," the killing of the firstborn of every household in Egypt.

Have students read Exodus 12:12–13. God outlines for Moses His final judgment on the Egyptians. The Israelites escape the angel of death by putting the blood of a Passover lamb on their doorframes (verse 13). God commands the Israelites to remember Passover as the day when God delivered them, or "passed over" their homes. He did not destroy their firstborn children.

GOD'S DELIVERANCE (15 minutes)

Have students read Romans 5:9–11 and answer the question on the student page. Their answers should reflect an understanding that the shedding of blood was required for the forgiveness of sin. The shedding of Christ's blood was the final sacrifice for the sins of all times. Read together Ephesians 1:7, and then list some similarities between the way God delivered the Israelites and the way He delivers us. Possibilities include the following:

Israelites
God's chosen people
Passover lamb
The blood of the Passover lamb assured that the angel of death would "pass over"

The Church
We are God's children in Baptism
Jesus is the Lamb of God
The blood of Jesus, our Lamb, saves us

DELIVERED BY GRACE (10 minutes)

Give students time to discuss with a partner the questions in this section. When one understands the Passover story, the Communion liturgy takes on new meaning. We are reminded that, because of Christ's blood shed for us, God "passes over" our sin and looks instead at the perfect sacrifice of His Son for us.

CLOSING (5 minutes)

Conclude by singing a Communion hymn, such as "O Jesus, Blessed Lord, To Thee" (*LSB* 632)/"O Jesus, Blessed Lord, My Praise" (*LW* 245).

LESSON EXTENDERS

✞ Have students compare and contrast Moses and Jesus. How was Moses' work like Christ's? As a leader, how was Moses similar to our Lord?

✞ Ask your pastor to take students on a "tour" to see the Communion vessels. Review the names of the vessels, why the Lord's Supper is important, and how it assures us of Christ's love.

GOD PASSES OVER

EGYPT'S SIN

Read **Exodus 12:12–13**. What did God tell Moses He would do to the Egyptians?

....

....

How could the Israelites be protected from the final plague?

....

....

After the event, God commands the Israelites to remember this day. Why is it called "Passover"?

....

....

GOD'S DELIVERANCE

The Bible is full of images that show the importance of blood. Why did Christ's sacrifice have to be bloody (see **Romans 5:9–11**)?

....

Read **Ephesians 1:7**. How are we redeemed by God?

....

List some similarities between the Passover for the Israelites and how God saves the church.

Israelites	**The Church**
....	....
....	....
....	....
....	....
....	....

DELIVERED BY GRACE

In the church service, when do you hear references to blood?

....

....

....

How can a reminder about Passover make this more meaningful for you?

....

....

....

....

....

Created in Christ © 2006 Concordia Publishing House. Reproduced by permission.

STUDENT PAGE 13

14. Great Escapes

Exodus 12:31–42; 13:17–15:21

Lesson Focus

Through Christ, God has a plan to rescue His children not only from the dangers of this life but also from death itself.

GREAT ESCAPE (10 minutes)

Distribute copies of Student Page 14. Ask for a volunteer to read the "Great Escape" story aloud. Ask the students to share a personal experience of when they escaped from a difficult situation. Your example might encourage others to share their stories. Challenge the students to think through their perception of dramatic rescues with the following questions: How might a Christian view a rescue differently than an unbeliever? (God's providence rather than luck) What should rescue experiences tell us about God's love and concern for us? (God does not desire to see us harmed.)

THE PLAN (15 minutes)

Great escapes are not new. The children of Israel experienced the power of God that rescued them from what seemed like an impossible situation.

If you have five or more students, divide the class into breakout groups. Allow students to work within their groups to uncover the surprises found in the texts. After ten minutes call the class back together and quickly compare the responses from each group. Possible responses: Surprise 1: God commanded the Israelites to leave a situation where they had been in bondage for four hundred years. Surprise 2: God's people not only left with the blessing of their captors but they took considerable wealth with them. Surprise 3: The Israelites were led by God in a cloud and pillar of fire.

Remind the students that God continued to bless His people. He protected them through forty years of wandering in the wilderness and delivered them safely to the Promised Land. God desires to protect us in our earthly wanderings and deliver us to His promised land of heaven.

THE GREATEST ESCAPE (20 minutes)

The apostle Paul was very aware of God's plan. Through the power of the Holy Spirit, he reveals it to us in the Book of Romans. Ask the students to move back into their groups and, using Romans 5:1–11 as a reference, respond to the questions on the student page.

Allow time for students to read the Scripture and respond to the questions. When you sense that the class has completed the assignment, call them together. Review their responses to the questions. Before concluding the lesson, pose the following questions: Why can we anticipate suffering? What does Paul have to say about earthly suffering? What is God's purpose in allowing suffering in our lives? Remind students that, while God has a plan to deliver us from death, that does not mean life on earth will be easy. Hope in God's deliverance in Christ sustains us.

CLOSING (5 minutes)

Remind the students that God promises to protect those who trust in Him. This does not mean there will not be suffering. Rather, it means that eternal life and deliverance from suffering await those who place their hope in Jesus Christ as their Savior.

Close the session with a circle prayer that all youth are not only kept safe from harm but that they might come to see Jesus as their only hope for salvation.

LESSON EXTENDERS

✝ In 2 Corinthians 11:21b–29, Paul talks about the various dangers he faced. Invite your students to read Paul's accounts. How do the dangers Paul faced compare to what contemporary teens face? What can we learn from Paul's experience and outlook on suffering?

Great Escapes

GREAT ESCAPE

Todd and Cliff were proud of the small sailboat they jointly owned. It was not uncommon for them to spend an entire summer day sailing on the large lake near their home. But neither of them was prepared for the sudden storm that came up one afternoon. The boys were in the middle of the lake when it appeared on the horizon. By the time they headed toward the shore it was too late. The small boat was no match for the high wind, and the mast was snapped in two. Twice the boat capsized in the fierce waves, but both times the boys managed to right it and crawl back on the deck. As they hung on for dear life, they discussed their chances of being rescued. First someone would have to discover that they were missing. After that a search party would have to be dispatched. The process could take at least an hour, and they were growing weaker by the minute. Todd was the first one to suggest that they pray. It was short and to the point: "God, please help us!" Within minutes the rain and wind began to let up. Shortly after the storm subsided, a Coast Guard helicopter appeared on the horizon. As it approached, the boys breathed a sigh of relief. They also wondered who had notified the rescue team and how they had found them so quickly on such a large body of water. Neither of them expected their prayers to be answered so dramatically.

THE PLAN

God had a plan for rescuing His people. He often works in surprising ways. The children of Israel discovered this when God rescued them from the Egyptians.

Surprise 1   **Exodus 12:31–34**

....

Surprise 2   **Exodus 12:35–36**

....

Surprise 3   **Exodus 13:20–21**

....

THE GREATEST ESCAPE

Read **Romans 5:1–11**.

What was God's escape plan for His people?

....

When and how was it accomplished?

....

What are the benefits awaiting those who have faith in God and do not reject His escape plan?

verse 1

....

verse 2

....

verses 3–5

....

verse 8

....

verse 11

....

15. IMPROPER PRAYERS

Exodus 16–17

Lesson Focus

God hears the prayers of His people and provides the best for us even when we pray with selfish motives or in "improper" ways.

MESSAGES AND MEANINGS (15 minutes)

In advance, prepare index cards with the following tasks on them. You will need one set of task cards for every two participants.

A. "Ask your partner for a pencil. Be as rude as you possibly can."
B. "Ask your partner to use his/her Bible. Be as polite as you can."
C. "Yelling loudly, ask your partner to borrow a piece of paper."
D. "With a big smile, ask your partner what time it is; then politely say thank you."

Divide students into pairs; if there is an uneven number, you will need to participate. Designate one person in each pair to go first. Give the first person in each pair cards A and B and the second person cards C and D. Have students take turns performing the tasks.

After every pair has completed all four tasks, distribute copies of Student Page 15 and have students individually complete the questions for this section. Have volunteers share their responses.

REQUESTING/RECEIVING (15 minutes)

Students should complete this section in pairs. Supply them with blank paper and markers or pencils. Have students follow the directions from the student page to complete this section.

Israel's requests:
Exodus 16:3—food
Exodus 17:3—water

God's gifts:
16:13–16—food (manna and quail)
17:6—water from a rock
17:10–13—defeat of their enemies (the Amalekites)

The Israelites complained and were demanding, which we would consider a rude way to "pray." Most people would not honor requests made in this way if given a choice. Also, Israel despised God's gift of food by not following His commands regarding the manna and the Sabbath (16:27–30). As learners share their drawings and responses to the questions, help them see that God gave these gifts to Israel because He loved them, not because they asked appropriately.

THE GIVER OF EVERY GOOD GIFT (15 minutes)

Each student should complete this section individually and then share with the group.

Ask students to list every gift they received from God in arrows pointing down. Give students three minutes to complete this task. Give two minutes for students to list things they've asked God for in the past week. You may need to provide ideas before getting started on each task. Have the group work together to complete a master list of blessings and requests.

As students compose their prayers for their greatest need, remind them of God's promise to hear all of our prayers, even if we pray with the wrong motive. Have a volunteer read Ephesians 3:20–21. With all that God has given us in the past, we can be confident that He will give us what is best in the future.

CLOSING (5 MINUTES)

Invite students to pray for each other's needs this week. Gather all the students in a circle and have them pass their paper to the person on their right. Go around the circle and read the prayers from activity 3. Close with your own prayer.

LESSON EXTENDERS

✠ Distribute a recent Sunday bulletin or newsletter. Have students list all the prayer needs they find. Have volunteers pray for those people.

✠ Ask students to monitor how they are asked to do things. Who is most rude in making requests of them: parents, teachers, siblings, or classmates?

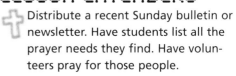

IMPROPER PRAYERS

MESSAGES AND MEANINGS

In one or two words describe *how* your partner asked you for something the first time.

In one or two words describe *how* your partner asked you for something the second time.

How do you *feel* when people ask you for things in a rude way?

How do you *feel* when people ask you for things in a polite or friendly way?

What is more important, *how* someone says something or what is said? Why?

REQUESTING/RECEIVING

In **Exodus 16–17** the Israelites asked God through Moses for two things. God answered their requests and then gave them something they didn't request. Read through these chapters and, on a separate sheet, draw a picture or write out a portion of Israel's prayers to God inside arrows pointing up. Draw or write out the gifts that God gave Israel in arrows pointing down.

Describe *how* the Israelites made their requests to God through Moses.

How would you have answered Israel's requests?

What else did the Israelites do to show that they didn't appreciate God's gifts?

THE GIVER OF EVERY GOOD GIFT

What do you need most in your life right now?

How does the Gospel of Jesus Christ meet your greatest need?

Write a prayer asking God to meet your need in the way that is best for you.

Created in Christ © 2006 Concordia Publishing House. Reproduced by permission.

STUDENT PAGE 15

16. THE ROAD TRIP

Numbers 21:4–9

Lesson Focus

Despite the complaining and lack of faith of the children of Israel in the wilderness, the Lord acts mercifully toward them. In the same way God shares His grace and mercy with us today.

ROAD TRIP SCRAPBOOK
(10 minutes)

Use a video clip from one of the Chevy Chase *Vacation* movies to show an uncomfortable, long drive, or recall a long road trip that you have taken. Ask, "What was the longest, most uncomfortable road trip you have ever taken? Did you complain to your parents or trip leaders? If so, what did you say? What was their response?"

OPENING UP SCRIPTURE
(10 minutes)

Hand out copies of Student Page 16. Read together Numbers 21:4–9. What were the people complaining about? (Being brought into the desert to die without food) What happened because of their complaining? (God sent venomous snakes among them.) What was the answer to their situation given by God to Moses? (To make a snake on a stick to be looked at for healing) How were the people saved? (By looking up at the snake)

DIGGING DEEPER
(10 minutes)

Read together John 3:14–15 and John 6:32–40. How do these verses bring a deeper understanding to what went on in the desert? (Christ is like the snake lifted up) How was Christ lifted up? (On the cross) What did the snake and Christ offer? (Life and salvation) How does Christ answer our needs? (Our ultimate need is an answer for the sin in our lives, and Christ died on the cross to remove the guilt of that sin.)

DRIVING IT HOME
(10 minutes)

What things do you complain about to God? (Answers will vary: money, looks, schoolwork.) How does God give an answer to each of your complaints? (Each problem should be answered in Christ; He fulfills all desires.) How can you lift your eyes to Christ in your life? (Being in the Word, worship, prayer, remembering your Baptism)

FINAL DESTINATION
(10 minutes)

Close by saying, "Sometimes we might feel as though we are on a journey that wanders with no direction. We might even complain to God that He is not meeting our needs. Jesus shows us that we often have our focus in the wrong direction and not on Him. In Jesus we have an answer to every desire, and we will know that fully when we reach our final destination of heaven." Close with prayer: "Heavenly Father, You are the Maker of all things and Creator of life. We know You have a map just for us. Forgive us for the times when we want to follow our own way rather than Yours. Thank You for Your guidance and direction. Please fill us with Your Spirit that we might live for You on this road of life and share the map with those around us. In Jesus' name. Amen."

LESSON EXTENDERS

✝ Have students reread John 6:32–40. What were the people asking for in the desert? (Food) How does Christ give an answer to the desire for food? (He is the bread of life; He satisfies all human desires.) How does looking up at the snake relate to Jesus? (He was on a cross; we look to Him for healing and salvation.) What significance is there in Jesus saying that He is the bread of life? (The children of Israel were begging for food; Jesus gives us spiritual food in Holy Communion.) Look at verse 40. What is it that saves us? (Looking to the Son and believing)

THE ROAD TRIP

OPENING UP SCRIPTURE

Read **Numbers 21:4–9**.

What were the people complaining about?

....

What happened because of their complaining?

....

What was the answer to their situation given by God to Moses?

....

....

How were the people saved?

....

....

DIGGING DEEPER

Read **John 3:14–15** and **John 6:32–40**.

How do these verses bring a deeper understanding to what went on in the desert?

....

....

What were the people asking for in the desert?

....

How does Christ give an answer to the desire for food?

....

How does looking up at the snake relate to Jesus?

....

....

....

DRIVING IT HOME

What things do you complain about to God?

....

....

....

How does God give an answer to each of your complaints?

....

....

....

How can you lift your eyes to Christ in your life?

....

....

....

Created in Christ © 2006 Concordia Publishing House. Reproduced by permission.

STUDENT PAGE 16

17. Letting God Lead

Joshua 3–4; 5:13–6:27

Lesson Focus

God uses events and trials in our lives to strengthen our faith and trust in Jesus as our Savior from sin.

LIVING BY THE LAW
(10 minutes)

Distribute copies of Student Page 17. Allow time for students to answer the questions. Discuss the consequences of breaking the rules in the given situations. Lead students to see that it is to our advantage to do what we know is right. Disobeying the rules or directions is part of our sinful nature and a way we rebel against God.

CROSSING THE RIVER
(20 minutes)

Allow students to work in breakout groups or pairs to answer the questions on the student page. Review their insights as a whole group.

The priests carrying the ark of the covenant were to enter the Jordan River first and stand there as the people passed by. Remind students that the ark of the covenant was not a magic box, but a symbol of the Lord's presence with Israel.

The water from upstream stopped flowing when the priests stepped into the river with the ark of the covenant. Even though the river was at flood stage, all the people were able to cross it on dry ground.

God performed this miracle to show His almighty power and to assure the people that they should put their trust in Him and not other gods like Baal, the god of the Canaanites.

TAKING THE CITY
(10 minutes)

Allow students to work in groups again to answer the student page questions. Review their answers.

All of Israel's armed men were to march around Jericho once a day for six days, following the ark of the covenant and seven priests carrying rams'-horn trumpets. On the seventh day they were to march around the city seven times while the priests blew the trumpets. They were to keep quiet until given a signal to shout.

The walls around Jericho fell down. The Israelites charged in and devoted the city to the Lord. Every living thing except for Rahab and her family was destroyed as God had commanded.

FOLLOWING JESUS
(5 minutes)

Complete and discuss the questions from the student page. Ask each student to respond to the second question.

Because of our sin, we deserve eternal death. But Jesus lovingly took the death penalty for us. He died, rose, and now gives us eternal life in heaven as a gift.

These stories remind us that God has a plan for our lives and He has the power and wisdom to carry it out. We should trust Him instead of relying on our own limited vision, knowing He will bring good from every situation (see Romans 8:28). Our obedience does not earn us anything, but by it we thank God for what He has done for us.

CLOSING **(5 minutes)**

Invite students to respond with "Lead me, Lord" after each phrase of the litany.

Dear Lord,

When I want to go along with the crowd instead of doing what I know is right . . .

When things are going well and I am tempted to rely on my own strength . . .

When I must make decisions about my future . . .

Thank You, Lord, that You lead us and will continue to do so. In Jesus' name we pray. Amen.

LESSON EXTENDERS

✝ What promises does God give us if we let Him lead? Will we be immune to troubles? See Isaiah 43:1–3; 48:10; and 2 Corinthians 12:7–10.

Letting God Lead

LIVING BY THE LAW

Who likes to follow directions? Who likes to break the rules? What are some of the rules for each of these settings? Why are they important? What rules don't make sense or seem fair? Why is it important in the following situations to follow directions, even when they don't make sense to you?

Playing on a basketball team

Checking in at the airport

Baby-sitting for your neighbor's infant

Giving medicine to someone who is ill

CROSSING THE RIVER

What directions were the people given in **Joshua 3:9–13**?

What happened when they followed the directions? See **Joshua 3:14–17**.

There were less dramatic ways that God could have gotten His people across the river. According to **Joshua 4:23–24**, what did He want them to know?

TAKING THE CITY

What directions were the people given in **Joshua 6:2–5**?

These commands must have seemed strange to the people, but they obeyed. What was the result? See **Joshua 6:15–21**.

FOLLOWING JESUS

God expects us to obey His commandments, but we have not done so. What is the consequence of our sin? What plan does God have to save us from our foolishness? See **Romans 6:23**.

How can the crossing of the Jordan River and the fall of Jericho encourage you when you are tempted to disobey seemingly foolish commands from God? See **Proverbs 3:5**.

Created in Christ © 2006 Concordia Publishing House. Reproduced by permission.

STUDENT PAGE 17

18. FOREIGNER NO MORE

The Book of Ruth

Lesson Focus

At some point in life, nearly everyone will experience the feeling of being a foreigner or outsider. Students will learn through this lesson that, out of His love and kindness, God welcomes all into the family of believers.

WHAT IS A FOREIGNER? (5 minutes)

List some times or places when someone might feel like an outsider. What does it feel like to be an outsider? Have you ever moved to a new community or been a newcomer among strangers? Describe the situation. Have students define the term *foreigner*. Share a time or situation in which you felt like a foreigner or outsider. Distribute copies of Student Page 18 and encourage students to complete the sentences. Invite volunteers to share their answers.

RUTH, THE FOREIGNER (15 minutes)

Use a map to show students the region of Moab in relation to Judah and the city of Bethlehem. Have individuals or groups read the Bible verses listed on the student page. Have volunteers share their responses to the questions. How does Boaz's response to Ruth compare to your experiences as an outsider?

GOD WELCOMES THE FOREIGNER (10 minutes)

Assign individuals or groups to read the Bible verses listed on the student page. Discuss how and what God provided for Ruth and Naomi. Read Isaiah 14:1 aloud. God provided not only for the needs of Ruth and Naomi, but made Ruth, a foreigner, one of the women in the family line of Jesus. Ruth's inclusion in the kingdom foreshadows the wide-open arms of Christ, welcoming all people of all nations who believe in Him.

WELCOMED INTO GOD'S KINGDOM (10 minutes)

Allow volunteers to read the selected Bible verses from Ephesians. Have students respond to the questions on the student page. Emphasize that, through the sacrifice of Jesus, the promises of God extend to everyone, not just the Jews. Discuss the imagery of a household (Ephesians 2:19) and a building whose stones rely first on Jesus, the "chief cornerstone," and then on the foundation, the Word of God.

WELCOMING OTHERS (10 minutes)

Discuss ways to welcome people of various cultures in your community to your church. Brainstorm ideas for reaching out to the community. Through faith in God and Baptism, we are welcomed into His family. We can approach each day renewed by the gift of forgiveness first given through our Baptism. Because of the kindness God has shown us, we can in turn welcome others.

CLOSING (5 minutes)

Encourage students to pray silently for the outreach ideas discussed during the lesson. Lead the class in this prayer: "Dear Jesus, I thank You for welcoming me into the kingdom of God. Forgive me for the times when I have not welcomed others. Please help me to reach out to others in love as You have reached out in love to me. In Your name I pray. Amen."

LESSON EXTENDERS

✞ How was growth in God's kingdom received by those who heard the preaching of the apostles? (See Acts 8:5–8; 8:26–39; 11:19–21; 14:1–4.)

✞ How did Jesus show acceptance of foreigners through His teaching (Luke 10:25–37; 17:11–19)?

FOREIGNER NO MORE

WHAT IS A FOREIGNER?

A foreigner is . . .

....

I have felt like a "foreigner" or outsider when . . .

....

....

When I was an outsider, people responded to me by . . .

....

....

RUTH, THE FOREIGNER

Where was Ruth from? Why did she leave her home (**Ruth 1:4–7; 11–19**)?

....

How did Boaz respond to Ruth, the foreigner (**Ruth 2:5–13**)?

....

GOD WELCOMES THE FOREIGNER

What and how did God provide for Ruth and her mother-in-law, Naomi (**Ruth 4:13–22**)?

....

Who else is in the family line of David (**Matthew 1:5–16**)?

....

....

WELCOMED INTO GOD'S KINGDOM

How does God welcome you into the family of believers (**Ephesians 2:12–13**)?

....

....

To what does Paul compare the family of believers? Why (**Ephesians 2:19–22**)?

....

....

WELCOMING OTHERS

How can we welcome others to the family of God (**Colossians 3:12–14; 4:2–6**)?

....

....

....

STUDENT PAGE 18

Created in Christ © 2006 Concordia Publishing House. Reproduced by permission.

19. Giving Back to God

1 Samuel 1

Lesson Focus

God gives us great gifts; His Spirit moves us to respond to His love for us by using these gifts to benefit the church and others.

OPENING (10 minutes)

Open with the video clip from *A Christmas Story* in which Ralphie finally gets the Red Rider BB gun he has been begging for. If that is not possible, give an example of a gift you were really hoping to receive. Ask, "What present did you really hope to get, and then finally got? What was your reaction to getting it?"

OPENING UP THE WORD (15 minutes)

Hand out copies of Student Page 19. Read 1 Samuel 1. Allow students to work individually to complete the questions. Discuss answers as a whole group. What is it that Hannah wants so badly? (A son) What makes her situation worse? (Her husband's other wife has children.) What is Hannah's request to God? (That she have a son, and she promised to give him to the Lord's work) What does Eli the priest think about Hannah when he sees her praying? (That she is drunk) What does Eli bless her with? (That God would give her what she desires) How does God honor Hannah's request? (A son is born to her.) How does Hannah honor God? (By dedicating Samuel to the Lord's work)

DIGGING DEEPER (15 minutes)

Allow students to work in breakout groups to complete this section. Discuss their answers as a whole group. How did Hannah demonstrate faithfulness to God before she had a son? (She offered sacrifices and prayed.) How did Hannah demonstrate that she knew her son was a gift from God? (She offered him to God's service with the priest.) What are similarities and differences between Jesus and Samuel? (*Similarities*: Jesus was dedicated to God's work; mother sang a song of joy; presented at the temple; long-awaited births. *Differences*: Hannah was married when Samuel was conceived; Samuel was not God; Samuel had an earthly biological father.)

BRINGING IT HOME (10 minutes)

Work as a whole group to study the verses and answer the questions in this section. Where do you go when you really want something? (Answers will vary.) Read John 6:68–69. How do you know that all good things come from God? (God promises this in His Word.) How can you give back to God what He has first given to you? (Only through the power of God's Spirit working in us are we able to bring our gifts of time, service, and treasure. It is solely a response to God's love shown to us.)

CLOSING (5 minutes)

Say, "The story of Samuel shows God's faithfulness to Hannah and reminds us of how God has provided for us in our lives. It also reminds us that God provided the long-awaited Savior, Jesus Christ, who served the Father by dying for us. Moved by the Holy Spirit, we show our gratitude to God in the same way that Hannah did—by offering our gifts in service to God." Pray, "Father in heaven, You are the source of all things good. You have given us all that we need for this life and for eternity. We confess that our wants are not always what You know we truly need. Forgive us for not taking care of the things You give us, and fill us with Your Spirit to serve You and dedicate all we have to You. In the name of Your most precious gift to us, Jesus, we pray. Amen."

Giving Back to God

OPENING UP THE WORD

Read **1 Samuel 1**.

What is it that Hannah wants so badly?

What makes her situation worse?

What is Hannah's request to God?

What does Eli the priest think about Hannah when he sees her praying?

What does Eli bless her with?

How does God honor Hannah's request?

How does Hannah honor God?

DIGGING DEEPER

How did Hannah demonstrate faithfulness to God before she had a son?

How did Hannah demonstrate that she knew her son was a gift from God?

What are similarities and differences between Jesus and Samuel?

BRINGING IT HOME

Where do you go when you really want something?

Read **John 6:68–69**. How do you know that all good things come from God?

How can you give back to God what He has first given to you?

Created in Christ © 2006 Concordia Publishing House. Reproduced by permission.

20. GOD'S PATIENCE

1 Samuel 8:1–11:15

Lesson Focus

God demonstrates His grace and patience with His people through the death and resurrection of Christ.

TOP FIVE (10 minutes)

Ask students to think of five things that non-Christian teens do because "everybody does it"—things Christian teens might *like* to do, but know they are not supposed to. List student responses on whiteboard or newsprint. Ask, "Why are Christians not supposed to do these things?" Give students a moment to share. Then ask, "When Christians do these things, does God always punish them? Why not? Why doesn't God punish us for every sin right away?" Allow the class to share for a few minutes, then transition into the study by saying something like, "Today's lesson offers us insights into how God deals with us when we go against His will."

ALL KINDS OF QUESTIONS (10 minutes)

As a class read 1 Samuel 8. Ask some students to summarize the story in their own words. Give students copies of Student Page 20, and invite them to review this section. Instruct students to work in pairs to look up the passages and answer the questions. What was wrong with the people wanting a king? (God Himself was to be their King.) Why would the people reject God as their King? (They were hard-hearted and sinful.) What was wrong with the people wanting to be like the other nations? (God had set them aside as His special people, called to be different, to give glory to Him.) Why did God allow them to have a king even though it was a sin? (God is patient and compassionate with sinful people.)

FOUR QUESTIONS FOR MY LIFE (15 minutes)

Ask students to review 1 Samuel 8 to reflect on questions found in this section of the student page. Encourage students to get personal and specific, using "I" and "me" rather than "we" and "us." Encourage them to share and discuss responses class members might have in common. (When you get to the fourth question, direct students' attention to the graphic on the student page and ask, "Why does Jesus on the cross represent God's patience?" Ask them to open their Bibles to 1 Timothy 2:3–6 for the answer. (God shows His patience by giving Jesus to die on the cross so that all people have the opportunity to come to a knowledge of the truth and be saved.)

REMEMBERING GOD'S PATIENCE (10 minutes)

Say something like, "When we remember that God is patient with us for our own good and salvation, it encourages us to live in gratitude for that patience." Ask students to think of examples of how God's patience helps them in their daily lives. (An example: "His patience helps me be patient with others.") Invite class members to think of a symbol that represents God's patience and forgiveness in their lives. An obvious one would be the cross, but encourage students to come up with additional ones that have a personal application.

Close your time together by having students recite the Lord's Prayer together.

LESSON EXTENDERS

✝ Invite students to search Psalm 103 to discover how God's patience is shown in a variety of ways.

GOD'S PATIENCE

ALL KINDS OF QUESTIONS

Look up the passages cited after each question to answer the questions.

What was wrong with the people wanting a king? **Judges 8:23; 1 Samuel 12:12; Isaiah 33:22**

....

....

Why would the people reject God as their King? **Zechariah 7:11–12; Romans 3:10–18**

....

....

What was wrong with the people wanting to be like the other nations? **Deuteronomy 7:1–9; 1 Peter 2:9**

....

....

Why did God allow them to have a king even though it was a sin? **Psalm 86:15; Romans 2:4; Romans 9:20–25**

....

....

Write a question from the Bible passages to ask your teacher and the rest of the class. Try to think of a Bible verse that will help others with the answer.

....

....

....

....

FOUR QUESTIONS FOR MY LIFE

1. Why does God want to be my King?

....

....

2. Why am I tempted to reject Him?

....

....

3. Why am I not supposed to be like everyone else?

....

....

4. Why does God allow sin?

....

....

STUDENT PAGE 20

Created in Christ © 2006 Concordia Publishing House. Reproduced by permission.

21. STEP-BY-STEP

1 Samuel 16:1–13

Lesson Focus

God tells Samuel to trust Him to show the way to the new king step-by-step. Even though there is potential danger involved, Samuel obeys. The Lord fulfills His word, just as He does when He asks us to obey.

WHERE ARE YOU GOING? (10 minutes)

Have a student volunteer choose another trustworthy student. The first student should be blindfolded at the doorway of the room. The second student should give step-by-step verbal instructions to the first student to guide him or her to a specific destination in the room. Be sure to serve as a "spotter" for the blindfolded student. After the volunteers have completed their task, distribute copies of Student Page 21 and discuss the questions with the whole group.

Answers will vary but may include difficulties avoiding obstacles and the insecurity of not being able to see what lies ahead. Students may express the feeling of not wanting to depend completely on another person.

WHO IS GIVING INSTRUCTIONS? (15 minutes)

Allow students to work together in small groups to read the selected verses from 1 Samuel and complete the questions from the student page. Discuss their findings as a whole group.

The Lord instructs Samuel to anoint the new king of Israel. Saul knows that God has chosen to replace him as king. Saul may try to kill Samuel if he finds out what Samuel is up to. Samuel does follow the Lord's instructions. God told him to take a heifer and say he had come to sacrifice to the Lord, to invite Jesse to the sacrifice, and then wait to be shown what to do. You can emphasize the danger Samuel faced and the faithfulness God helped him show.

A LIGHT FOR MY PATH . . . NOT ALWAYS THE WHOLE HIGHWAY! (15 minutes)

A lamp or candle with a flame will work best for this activity, but a small flashlight will work in a pinch. Turn off all the lights, and light a lamp or candle. Have the person holding the light take one step and then several more. Discuss the questions from the student page as a whole group.

The point is that the light only illuminates an area immediately around the person holding it. The distance illuminated ahead of the person will remain the same no matter how far he or she walks. Samuel also "saw" only right in front of him. Point out that God works through His Word and Sacraments to strengthen our faith and trust in Him. Studying past examples of the Lord's faithfulness helps to encourage us that He will fulfill His promises to us.

CLOSING (10 minutes)

Encourage the group to participate in the prayer. If they are not comfortable praying out loud, you may have them write specific requests on index cards, and you can lead the prayer.

LESSON EXTENDERS

✝ Read a newsletter from a missionary or invite missionaries or other professional church workers to come in and share how they were called to their work and how they are able to follow the Lord's leading.

Step-by-Step

WHERE ARE YOU GOING?

Why might it be difficult for the blindfolded person to get to the destination?

Even if you were able to choose the person you trust most to give you instructions, why might it be difficult to trust that person completely?

WHO IS GIVING INSTRUCTIONS?

Read **1 Samuel 16:1–3**.

What honorable task is the Lord instructing Samuel to do?

What reason does Samuel have to be afraid?

Read **verse 4**. Did Samuel follow instructions? How many instructions was he given at one time?

Do you think you would have followed instructions in the same circumstances? Explain.

A LIGHT FOR MY PATH . . . NOT ALWAYS THE WHOLE HIGHWAY!

How far in front of you does the light shine?

How far ahead does the light shine after taking a step?

How far ahead will the light shine when you have taken one hundred steps?

Read **Psalm 119:105**. This verse doesn't say you will see the whole highway. How far ahead did Samuel "see" (in the instructions he was given)?

What can help you trust God enough to take the next step He is showing you?

Created in Christ © 2006 Concordia Publishing House. Reproduced by permission.

22. Real Friendship

1 Samuel 17:55—20:42;
2 Samuel 1:1—17

Lesson Focus

Friendship is a wonderful gift from God. The source and strength for Jonathan and David's friendship was their trust in God. As students explore this friendship, they will find strength in Jesus' love for friendships of their own.

OPENING (5 minutes)

Before class, draw a large copy of the chart in section 1 of the student page on the board or newsprint. As students arrive, greet them and ask who their best friends are. Ask them to list as many best friends whom they have had over the years as they can remember.

Ask the students to brainstorm five qualities that describe a best friend. (Students could work in pairs or teams of three.) When most have finished, ask volunteers to share one or more qualities from their lists. Ask how many others listed that quality and write the most common ones diagonally on the top of your large copy of the chart. Compliment the students on their choices.

BIBLE SEARCH (15 minutes)

Distribute copies of Student Page 22. Have the students transfer the five most common traits of friends to the top of their student page charts. Remind the students of the great friendship between Jonathan (King Saul's son and heir-apparent to the throne) and David (the shepherd-boy-turned-soldier and king-designate). Assign the students (individually, in pairs, or in teams of three) to read one of the five passages on the chart, watching for and marking the friendship qualities they have listed. After ten minutes, invite reports on each passage and mark the large chart.

THE SOURCE (15 minutes)

Read and discuss the two questions below the chart. Among the incredible aspects of this friendship is the reality that Jonathan might have expected to become king after his father rather than David. God enabled Jonathan to trust God's choice, allowing this friendship to exist and grow. As you discuss the second question, point out that, because we are all sinful, our friendships will fall apart unless, by God's grace, we approach each other with unconditional love. God's love is the source and strength of our love for others (1 John 4:19). Then ask the students to consider and discuss the following statements:

- Love is commitment.
- Love is not emotion but action.
- Love is a decision.
- Jesus is God's love.

WE ARE GOD'S FRIENDS (10 minutes)

Read these additional Bible passages that reflect God's friendship in Jesus. Invite students to choose their favorite and mark it in their Bibles. Invite volunteers to share their choices and reasons for them.

CLOSING (5 minutes)

Invite the students to identify one really great blessing God provides in their current friendships. Provide blank paper and have them write a note of thanks to a friend. Encourage them to share these notes with their friends, but don't require sharing in class. Close with prayer.

LESSON EXTENDERS

✞ Discuss: With whom could Jesus be leading you to establish a new friendship in the spirit of Jonathan and David?

✞ What benefits are yours through friendship with Jesus Christ? List them. Brainstorm ways to share them with your other friends.

Real Friendship

BIBLE SEARCH

Read the following passages from the account of Jonathan and David. Check the qualities you find in their friendship on the chart.

1 Samuel 17:57–18:4 "The Prince and the Giant-Slayer Become Friends"					
1 Samuel 18:27–19:3 "King Saul Becomes Jealous"					
1 Samuel 19:4–7 "Jonathan Stands Up for David"					
1 Samuel 19:16–23 "I Promise"					
2 Samuel 1:17–27 "Jonathan Is Dead"					

THE SOURCE

From what you have read and heard, what made the friendship between David and Jonathan so incredible?

....

In what way are Christian friendships based on unconditional love?

....

....

....

WE ARE GOD'S FRIENDS

Jesus is the best, and, in fact, only example of someone who has perfect, unconditional love for you. The following passages are examples of that love. Read them and choose your favorite.

☐ **Romans 5:8**

☐ **Ephesians 5:1–2**

☐ **1 John 4:10–11**

23. Cleaning Up Your Act

2 Samuel 11:1–12:14

Lesson Focus

Despite David's relationship with God, he fell deeply into sin. The Lord, in His great mercy, forgave David's repentant heart, just as His gracious forgiveness is given to His children today.

Note to teacher:
It is often easy to focus on the act of adultery in the story of David and Bathsheba, particularly in a group of teens. Many are likely to be unaware of the extent to which David tried to cover up his crime and how honorably Uriah behaved. They are even less likely to be aware of the process God used to bring David to repentance and restoration as His forgiven child—definitely a more important theme than the sin itself!

YOU DID A BAD, BAD THING! (5 minutes)

Distribute copies of Student Page 23. Ask students to read the scenario and possible responses. Allow students the opportunity to share their responses and the reasons behind them.

FROM BAD TO WORSE (10 minutes)

Have students work together in breakout groups to read the text and respond to the questions. Possible answers include the following:

David saw Bathsheba, lusted after her, then sent for her to sleep with him—a deliberate action into sin. Old Testament law stated that both parties involved in adultery should be put to death. Uriah said he would feel guilty enjoying the comforts of home while his comrades were living in tents at war. David was doing exactly that—even enjoying Uriah's wife. Uriah's high degree of honor contrasts sharply with David's despicable acts. After failing to get Uriah to go home and sleep with Bathsheba so that it would appear that the baby was Uriah's, David arranged for Uriah to be killed on the front lines of battle. David's desperation to escape the consequences of his sin may be one explanation. Students should be reminded that with God's power, the believer can flee temptation (James 4:7).

YOU'RE THE MAN! (10 minutes)

Have students return to their groups to complete this section. Discuss their findings.

"But the thing David had done displeased the Lord" (v. 27). The parable Nathan told set up a parallel situation for David's actions that David would see as despicable. In condemning the man in the parable, David was actually condemning himself. You may point out that he does not use excuses, rather his words indicate a contrite heart. God's response through Nathan was that the Lord had taken away David's sin and that he would not die.

THE BIG BUT (10 minutes)

Read and discuss as a whole group. Verse 14 indicates that, because of David's actions, the son he conceived with Bathsheba in adultery would die. There were other consequences as well, which play out in the continuation of 2 Samuel. Emphasize that David's consequences do not indicate incomplete forgiveness from the Lord.

YOU, TOO, CAN BE FORGIVEN! (10 minutes)

Students' reactions to the statements and questions will vary, but are likely to include the negative consequences of sin and the importance of confession and repentance. Answers are likely to include the assurance of forgiveness and grace for the repentant, even in the case of very "big" sins.

Pray together, thanking the Lord for His merciful forgiveness and asking for His help in resisting temptations.

Cleaning Up Your Act

YOU DID A BAD, BAD THING!

You have cheated in school. You work harder than you had studied to keep your actions secret. Before long, though—despite your best efforts—your teacher confronts you about your action. How are you most likely to respond?

- ☐ Confess and accept full responsibility for your actions.
- ☐ Make an excuse about all the pressure you have been under.
- ☐ Make an excuse about how hard the course is and how hard the teacher's tests are.
- ☐ Try to implicate your innocent friend as an accessory so you don't look quite so bad.

FROM BAD TO WORSE

Read **2 Samuel 11:1–27**.

What were David's first steps into this sin?

Why did David and Bathsheba work so hard on the cover-up?

Why does the fact that Uriah wouldn't go home make David look even worse?

What does David resort to when that plan fails?

Why do you think David got so out of control?

YOU'RE THE MAN!

Read **2 Samuel 11:27–12:14**.

What statement shows God's view about what David had done?

How does the parable Nathan tells "set David up"?

What is David's response (**verse 13**)?

What is God's response?

THE BIG BUT

Read **2 Samuel 12:13–14**.

What consequences did David still experience, even though God had forgiven him?

Are you more likely to accept or resent consequences when you have been told you are forgiven (from your parents, for example)?

YOU, TOO, CAN BE FORGIVEN!

Please notice that David sinned some very "big" sins. Not only did he commit adultery, but he also committed murder in an attempt to cover it up. Yet God forgave his repentant heart. What does this mean?

What lessons does the Lord provide for your life through this story?

What comfort does the Lord provide for your life through this story?

STUDENT PAGE 23

Created in Christ © 2006 Concordia Publishing House. Reproduced by permission.

24. GOD'S HOUSE

1 Kings 5–8

Lesson Focus
God wills for us to set aside times and places for worship, both for our good and His glory.

OPENING (10 minutes)

Before class, prepare some slips of paper on which are written the names of various objects found in your church building (altar, organ, cross, etc.). If your group is large, you may want to split into smaller groups. One student should choose a slip and draw a picture of the object on a chalkboard or large sheet of paper. The rest of the group will try to guess what object is being drawn. When you have finished drawing and guessing all of the objects, ask students to identify the common theme that these objects share.

SOLOMON'S JOB (5 minutes)

Distribute copies of Student Page 24. Ask a volunteer to read 1 Kings 5:1–5. Discuss the questions from the student page as a whole group. God had planned for Solomon to build the temple. Focus on the great privilege Solomon felt at being chosen to direct the building of the temple.

THEN AND NOW (15 minutes)

(Note: The text has been shortened to allow for completion in one class period. It is strongly suggested, however, that the leader read the entire text ahead of time.) Have students work together in breakout groups to fill in the two columns on the student page. The Bible references contain many descriptions—students will note those items that capture their attention. If time or attention is short, you might want to divide the references into smaller sections for breakout groups or individuals. While many of the objects described have counterparts in the contemporary church, remind students that one thing they won't see in a church today is an altar of sacrifice like was used in Old Testament times. Christ's death was the final sacrifice. By the power of His resurrection, we have been given eternal life with Him in heaven.

PRIORITIES AND PURPOSES (15 minutes)

Work through the questions on the student page as a group.

Solomon built God's house first—a reminder that God is to have priority in our lives. Solomon speaks much of God's fulfillment of His promises—a fact on which we also can rely. "All the peoples of the earth may know that the Lord is God and that there is no other." Solomon had a mission—just as Christ gave us—to spread the news of God's love.

Discuss the last two questions with the students. Guide them to focus on the importance of worship and to realize that corporate worship is pleasing to God. It is in corporate worship that we hear and learn God's Word, receive the Sacraments for forgiveness and the strengthening of our faith, and have the opportunity to respond to God in prayer and praise.

CLOSING (5 minutes)

Read and pray together 1 Kings 8:23.

LESSON EXTENDERS

✞ Many Bibles, such as the *Concordia Self-Study Bible*, include artists' renditions of the temple. Have students compare these with the text or draw their own diagrams and sketches.

✞ Students may find it interesting to visit various church buildings and discuss the similarities and differences from their own church and/or the temple.

GOD'S HOUSE

SOLOMON'S JOB

Solomon was given a special job to do. Read **1 Kings 5:1–5**. What was that job? Who commanded it?

....

....

....

THEN AND NOW

Make a list of things that can be found in our church building.

....

....

....

....

Use the Scripture references to make a list of things that describe the temple Solomon built.
1 Kings 6:14–38

....

....

....

....

1 Kings 7:13–51

....

....

....

....

PRIORITIES AND PURPOSES

Chapter 7 tells us that Solomon built his palace after he built the temple. Why do you think he built the temple first?

....

....

Read the beginning of Solomon's prayer of dedication in **1 Kings 8:22–24**. What does Solomon say about God?

....

....

Now read Solomon's message to the people in **1 Kings 8:56–61**. What did Solomon want "all the peoples of the earth [to] know" (**verse 60**)?

....

....

How does that compare to Jesus' words to us in **John 3:16**?

....

....

Solomon's temple was probably grander than we can imagine. We build our churches to be beautiful places. Why do we place value on building such great structures?

....

....

Why do we place a lot of emphasis on corporate (group) worship?

....

....

Created in Christ © 2006 Concordia Publishing House. Reproduced by permission.

25. VICTORY!

1 Kings 18:16–19:18

Lesson Focus

Through this study participants will praise God for the victory of Christ over sin, death, and the devil and trust Him to bring victories in their daily lives.

CENTRAL EAGLES WIN STATE (15 minutes)

After an opening prayer, distribute copies of Student Page 25. Ask a volunteer to read aloud "Central Eagles Win State." Invite teams of students to create stationary tableaus illustrating this or other common "victories" of teenagers. Then interview participants in the tableau with questions like, "How did it feel . . . ? To what do you attribute . . . ?" List these and other victories on the board. After everyone has shared, erase or draw a line through each example. Remind the students that most earthly accomplishments are soon forgotten, but God leads us in spiritual victories of eternal value.

ELIJAH'S GREAT VICTORY (25 minutes)

Divide the students into groups of about five. Have each group appoint a reader and a person to record the answers. Direct them to 1 Kings 18:16–40. As they read the story, the other members of the group should follow along in their Bibles, watching for the correct responses to questions on the student page. After about ten minutes, ask groups to share their responses. The correct answers are

- Opponents: the prophets of Baal
- Battlefield: Mount Carmel
- Strategy: to trust in God
- How achieved: God sent fire to consume Elijah's offering, while the Baal prophets failed
- Effect: the false prophets were slaughtered

Ask a volunteer to read aloud 1 Kings 19:1–18 for the entire group. Ask each small group to discuss the questions on the student page.

After about three minutes, ask groups to share their responses. Conclude the activity by saying, "Elijah's victory did not bring the expected results. He ended up a marked man. His life was in jeopardy. He learned that earthly victories are temporary, but God continues to lead and bless those whom He loves."

OUR VICTORIES (10 minutes)

Remind the class, "While earthly victories are soon forgotten, Jesus has won victories for us with eternal value." Direct the students to this section of the student page. Ask them to work independently, locating the Bible passages and recording their response. Give them five minutes to work, then ask individuals to share their responses. (Victory No. 1—over death; Victory No. 2—over the devil; Victory No. 3—over the temptations of the world)

CLOSING (5 minutes)

Have a student read aloud Romans 8:37. Then say, "Because of Jesus' suffering and death, we can face and conquer any earthly obstacle. Those who trust in Jesus Christ as their Savior have eternal victory in heaven." Close with prayer. Include a petition that God, through the power of the Holy Spirit, would bless each class member as conquerors in Jesus' name.

LESSON EXTENDERS

✝ Discuss what advice students might give a friend who is successful in many things (good grades, nice home, etc.) but still not happy.

VICTORY!

CENTRAL EAGLES WIN STATE

The Central High School Eagles capped off their dream season by soundly defeating Lincoln High School 35–0 in the State Championship Game. Quarterback Del Smith threw for three first-half touchdowns, leading the team to a 28–0 halftime lead. Running back Max Jones rushed for 179 yards and two touchdowns. Following the game, Smith and Jones shared the honors as the game's Most Valuable Players. Both young men have been offered football scholarships to attend State University next fall. When asked for his comments on the team's undefeated season, coach Buz Kutt stated, "This was a real team effort. The guys really worked hard and proved that they are the best team in the state. They deserve all the credit we can give them."

ELIJAH'S GREAT VICTORY

Read **1 Kings 18:16–40**.

Who was the opponent?

Where was the battlefield?

What was Elijah's strategy?

How was the victory achieved?

What effect did the victory have?

Read **1 Kings 19:1–18**.

How did the victory affect Elijah's life?

What lessons did Elijah learn?

OUR VICTORIES

1 Corinthians 15:26—Victory No. 1

Hebrews 2:14—Victory No. 2

1 John 5:4—Victory No. 3

26. Something So Simple

2 Kings 5:1–19

Lesson Focus

As God works through simple and humble means, we are reminded that all power is His alone.

FIRST AID (10 minutes)

Distribute copies of Student Page 26. Ask the students to complete the list of simple first-aid supplies or procedures. You may add items they didn't mention, such as antibiotics, ice, and such. Bring out the idea that sometimes very simple methods (ice, pressure on a cut) can be very effective treatments.

NAAMAN'S HELP FOR HEALING (20 minutes)

Have the students read 2 Kings 5:1–19. Work through the questions, focusing on these points:

Though Naaman was a powerful soldier, no one would have wanted to trade places with him because of his skin condition.

Levitical law called for examination by the priests, isolation from others, and ritual cleansing. Because Naaman was not from Israel, he was probably not subject to these rules. Some scholars question whether Naaman had modern leprosy (Hansen's disease), which would have severely limited his social contact, or another skin condition. Either way, life was difficult for him because of it.

Jewish servant girl: Prompts Naaman to seek healing from the prophet in her homeland.

King of Aram (Ben-Hadad II): Writes a letter of introduction and requests help for his servant Naaman.

King of Israel (Joram): The faithless king fears that Naaman is leading a military raid on Israel. He suspects Naaman has political motives rather than a desire for godly healing. He probably became suspicious of betrayal by Elisha.

Elisha: God's humble servant in faith sends Naaman to wash in the Jordan, trusting God's power to cleanse and heal.

Naaman's servants: Rather than agreeing with Naaman's indignity, his servants encourage Naaman to follow the instructions given by Elisha.

Naaman was looking for a supernatural or ritual healing; instead, he was told to wash in the muddy Jordan River. Elisha wanted Naaman to realize that the power to heal was not his own, but God's. Naaman pledges to worship the true God only and tries to give Elisha the gifts he has brought, which Elisha refuses.

A SERVANT OF GOD (10 minutes)

This section helps students focus on the simple and humble means God uses to show His power. Remind students that God has power and dominion over everything.

Christ was sent to be our ultimate servant, to give His life that we might be saved. This is a good time to remind students that our good works do not gain our salvation. Only Christ's death and resurrection, which we receive as a gift through faith, saves us.

Encourage students to seriously consider the wonder of Christ's sacrifice for us and their response as God's servants.

CLOSING (5 minutes)

Close by praying for God's guidance and encouragement in our roles as His servants. If the song is familiar, join in singing "Make Me a Servant" (*AGPS* 174).

LESSON EXTENDERS

✝ Think of other biblical examples of ways in which God used humble people and simple things to fulfill His purposes.

Something So Simple

FIRST AID

Make a list of things that might be found in a first-aid kit. How are these items used to help heal an illness or injury?

....

....

NAAMAN'S HELP FOR HEALING

Read **2 Kings 5:1–19**. The Scripture verses tell us that the Lord gave Naaman victory in battle, but Naaman had a problem. What was it?

....

How would this condition be treated in Jewish society? (See **Leviticus 13:2–8; 14:8–9**.)

....

God works through a variety of people to bring about healing for Naaman. What role did each of the following people play?

Jewish servant girl

....

King of Aram

....

King of Israel

....

Elisha

....

Naaman's servants

....

Why was Naaman upset by Elisha's instructions? What kind of healing was he looking for?

....

How is Naaman affected by this encounter with Elisha?

....

A SERVANT OF GOD

God often works through simple means (such as the water of Baptism). The water and the servants were important parts of the story, but from where did the power come?

....

Read **2 Peter 1:3**. What has God's power given us?

....

Who was sent to be our ultimate servant?

....

Read **Matthew 20:28**. For what twofold purpose was Christ sent?

....

Why is that so important?

....

Because of our salvation we can live as God's joyful servants. Think for a moment about the awesome opportunity it is to be God's servant. Make a list of ways you can serve.

....

Created in Christ © 2006 Concordia Publishing House. Reproduced by permission.

27. Spiritual Sickness

2 Kings 11:1–12:21

Lesson Focus

This study will help students recognize their sin, rejoice that God has called them through His Son, Jesus Christ, and respond to their salvation by putting faith into action.

OPENING (5 minutes)

Have students list symptoms of the flu or a cold. Remind students, "Flu, colds, and other viruses cannot be cured with medicine, but the symptoms can be treated. The same is true for sin. The symptoms can be dealt with, but we are never cured of sin until we enter eternity through Jesus Christ."

SIN SICKNESS (30 minutes)

Distribute copies of Student Page 27 and have students fill in the chart as follows:

2 Kings 11–12: Have the students read 2 Kings 11:1–12:21 and record people and their sin-symptoms on the chart. People and symptoms include Athaliah—murder (11:1); Jehoiada—violent coup (11:4–21); the priests—lax religious service (12:6) and misappropriation of funds (12:8); Joash—political conspiracy (12:18); and Joash's officials—murder and violent coup (12:20).

Society Today: Clip newspaper stories that show symptoms of sin in society and tape them on a wall or discuss recent examples. Again invite the students to identify individuals and the indications of sin in these examples. Have them complete that section of the student page chart.

My Personal Life: Allow students time to think about the symptoms of sin among their family and friends (in school, work, home life, athletics, dating, and the like). Have them add these to their chart. Invite discussion only if your students trust one another and will keep confidences.

PRESCRIPTION: CHRIST (15 minutes)

Read the opening paragraph. Point out the diagnosis common to all three "Symptoms" sections on the chart: sick with sin. Have the students enter the diagnosis on the chart, then discuss the questions on the student page, incorporating these comments:

1. 1 Peter 2 speaks of those who were "not a people" becoming God's people, those who were lost in sin and "without mercy" receiving God's mercy. Those whom God loves, including you and me, are transformed from people sick with sin to God's righteous saints. In 2 Kings 11–12, Joash demonstrates this transformation under the godly instruction of Jehoiada. It happens in our lives as we hear the Gospel and grow in faith.

2. 1 Peter 2:12 instructs Christians to "live such good lives among the pagans that, though they accuse you of doing wrong, they may see your good deeds and glorify God on the day He visits us." Lead the class to identify specific actions applicable to their lives.

3. Answers will vary, but could include submitting to the authority of parents, supporting and witnessing to friends, and serving others in love. Help the students be specific.

4. Answers could include Christian friends, worship, Bible study, prayer, personal devotions, family devotions, and the like.

CLOSING (5 minutes)

Ask for prayer requests and close with prayer.

LESSON EXTENDERS

✝ Create a list of social ministries in your area and covenant as a class to be involved with these ministries during the Thanksgiving and Christmas seasons.

✝ Encourage students to make a plan for personal study of Scripture and prayer. Have students pair up and be accountable to each other for worship, Bible class, and prayer.

Spiritual Sickness

SIN SICKNESS

Patient	Symptoms	Diagnosis	Rx
2 Kings 11–12			☧
Society Today			☧
My Personal Life			☧

PRESCRIPTION: CHRIST

The symptoms of spiritual sickness are very evident—in Scripture, in society, and in our lives. They are an indication of a life-threatening problem—sin. The prescription is simple: Christ. (The Chi-Rho is a symbol for Christ made up of the first two Greek letters in the Greek word for Christ.)

Read **1 Peter 2:4–12**. Then respond to these questions.

1. How does this passage describe the transformation from spiritual sickness to health?

2. To what Christian actions are you called as an individual member of the body of Christ, and as a member of today's society?

3. Describe your calling as a chosen one of God—a teenager, son/daughter, or sibling. What responsibilities does your call carry? What privileges do you enjoy?

4. What tools and experiences has God provided to assist you in responding to His call? How well do you use them?

STUDENT PAGE 27

Created in Christ © 2006 Concordia Publishing House. Reproduced by permission.

28. PROMISES & TRUST

2 Kings 18:1–20:11

Lesson Focus

Hezekiah trusted in God's protection even when everything around him seemed to spell disaster. When we find ourselves in difficult situations, we can trust God to sustain us, regardless of the distress.

OPENING (5 minutes)

Place a chair in front of the group and encourage students to talk about it. Ask questions such as, "Do you think this chair will hold you if you sit on it? Are you sure? What makes you so sure? What if the screws and bolts that hold it together are loose?" Ask a volunteer to sit on the chair, and talk about times when it is difficult to trust other people. Ask how and why the students trust you.

HEZEKIAH: A TRUSTING KING (15 minutes)

Distribute copies of Student Page 28. Encourage a volunteer to read aloud the short background information. Then take turns reading the two chapters from 2 Kings. In pairs, have the students look at the descriptive words for Hezekiah and God and identify supporting verses from the reading. Answers may vary; accept them when defensible. Emphasize Hezekiah's trust in God's promises and God's long history of faithfulness and dependability to His chosen people.

OUR TRUSTWORTHY GOD (15 minutes)

Allow students to consider why dependability is an important human characteristic and then contrast our human weakness with God's steady and sure reliability. Student suggestions will vary. Lead the conversation so that reliability is seen as a valuable asset. Students will find many descriptions of God's dependability as they read Psalm 46 and complete the activity. Phrases may include "refuge," "strength," and "ever-present help."

ME: A TRUSTING FAITH (15 MINUTES)

Invite students to share why they responded to each situation the way they did. Following the questions on the student page, lead a discussion about trust. Emphasize that often it is our slowness to believe in God's mercy that prevents us from enjoying the full reassurance God wants for us. Sin often leads us to doubt our gracious God, yet Christ died for our sins of unbelief too. Ask two volunteers to reread portions of the Scripture concerning Hezekiah specified on the student page. Discuss the questions and help students to understand the reassurance God gives us in His Word that a prayer, made in faith, is heard and answered.

CLOSING (5 minutes)

Read responsively Psalm 62:5–8. Have students finish the statement "God is a refuge for me when _____."

LESSON EXTENDERS

✝ Have students explore other verses that demonstrate God's trustworthy nature: Joseph in Egypt, Genesis 45:4–7; Paul's assurance, Romans 8:28.

Promises & Trust

HEZEKIAH: A TRUSTING KING

Prior to what is recorded in this passage, the King of Assyria had conquered all of Israel. Hezekiah was a king of Judah, to the south, the only remaining portion of the Promised Land inhabited by God's chosen people.

After reading **2 Kings 18–19**, choose two of the following descriptive words each for Hezekiah and God. Which words are accurate descriptions? List at least two verses that support your choices.

Hezekiah		God
	Faithful	
	Dependable	
	Indecisive	
	Unconcerned	
	Confused	
	Impatient	
	Obedient	
	Trustworthy	

OUR TRUSTWORTHY GOD

What are some characteristics of people who are not dependable? When wouldn't you want to work with an unreliable person?

....

....

Read **Psalm 46**. List the phrases that describe God as trustworthy.

....

....

....

....

ME: A TRUSTING FAITH

In which of the following situations do you think it would be most difficult to trust in God?

....

When you sin and struggle with guilt?

....

When none of your friends go to church?

....

When you have family problems?

....

Other

....

When we hold onto our doubts, fears, and worries, we deny ourselves the peace God gives us as we trust Him. Jesus, our promised Savior, forgives us for our lack of faith as He works repentance within us.

Read **2 Kings 19:15–19; 20:1–3**. What does Hezekiah do in times of trouble? What can you do in times of difficulty?

....

....

29. PREPARING FOR GOD'S PLAY

Esther

Lesson Focus

Young people may think they are too young to serve God. This lesson helps them see that God has work for them to do here and now. God's will is done with or without them! He desires to involve them and share His blessings with them.

OPENING (5 minutes)

Pass around some newsmagazines that focus on celebrities. Have students identify signs of good and bad in the celebrities' lives. Ask for other examples of people who were in the right place at the right time and became famous. What led to their fame? How is God involved when things look like luck or coincidence?

PREPARING FOR THE TASK (10 minutes)

Distribute copies of Student Page 29. Ask students to respond to the choices on the student page. Then pose these questions:

- An athlete trains rigorously but sits on the bench. A fellow bench-sitter skips practices, then gripes that the coach is unfair. When an injured player needs replacing, which one of the bench-sitters do you think will be picked to play? Why?
- A musician practices several hours a day, dreaming of a solo opportunity. A fellow musician with much natural talent does not practice. Which do you think the music director will choose for the solo? Why?
- A medalist swimmer watches as someone struggles against the deadly current of the river. He has the ability to make the rescue, but he is not willing to do so. Would you risk your life to save someone you didn't know? Why?

Conclude by asking, "How might God lead a believer to act in each situation? What do Colossians 3:17 and Romans 12:3–8 say about our attitude and action in life situations?"

LOOKING INTO GOD'S WORD (20 minutes)

Class time will not allow for reading all ten chapters of the Book of Esther. However, the instructor should be familiar with the entire story.

The story line should be easily understood by reading the following sections: 2:1–7, 17–23; 3:1–2, 5–6; and 4:1–17. Volunteers can read aloud or present a class drama with parts for a narrator, Haman, Mordecai, Esther, and King Xerxes.

Have students share their answers to the questions from the student page.

Focus on Esther 4:12–14. Discuss students' answers to the questions on the student page.

CARRYING OUT THE TASK (10 minutes)

Help students see their place in God's plan. Ask, "Is it coincidence that you are a Christian? Is it fate that you live where you live? Is it luck that your friends have you as a friend? How does God motivate Christians to meet others' needs? How does God equip believers for service to Him?"

Ask students to write down a friend's name on the student page. Remind them that this friend was put in their life by God's design. What does this friend need? Does this friend know Jesus as Savior? How can your students help? Fear may prevent us from serving others in God's name as led by the Holy Spirit. Have the class read 2 Timothy 1:7. Discuss how Jesus' grace overcomes fear. Discuss how 2 Timothy 2:20–21 describes us as God's instruments.

CLOSING (5 minutes)

Invite students to pray for a friend. Have them ask for the Holy Spirit's guidance in discovering how God can use them to serve their friends and others.

LESSON EXTENDERS

✝ Encourage students to write a list of strengths that God has blessed them with. Challenge them to be sensitive to their friends' needs and to consider how God desires to use them to share blessings with others.

Preparing for God's Play

PREPARING FOR THE TASK

Circle those things that you feel lead to success.

luck	timing	good looks
location	coincidence	power
training	availability	position
God	fate	money
practice	recognition	friends

How does God define success? (See **Matthew 16:24–26**.)

....

....

What do **Colossians 3:17** and **Romans 12:3–8** say about our attitude and action in life situations?

....

....

....

LOOKING INTO GOD'S WORD

Turn to the Old Testament Book of **Esther**. Read **2:1–7**, **17–23**; **3:1–2, 5–6**; and **4:1–17**.

• What was Haman's evil plan?

....

• What was God's plan in this evil situation?

....

Look closely at **Esther 4:12–14**.

• How did Mordecai show faith that God would rescue the Jews?

....

• Was it coincidence that Esther was on the throne?

....

• What would God have done if Esther had remained silent?

....

• Whose power alone can overcome evil?

....

• In what ways was Esther's an earthly success story? In what ways might it be a spiritual success story?

....

....

....

CARRYING OUT THE TASK

God has given me a friend whose name is _____

My friend knows/does not know Jesus as Savior. _____

My friend has this special need: _____

2 Timothy 1:7 reminds me: _____

I also remember God's purpose for my life (**2 Timothy 2:20–21**).

....

....

STUDENT PAGE 29

Created in Christ © 2006 Concordia Publishing House. Reproduced by permission.

30. Idol Nonsense

Daniel 3:1–30

Lesson Focus

In the beginning, God created people in His own image. In our sin, we tend to fashion or choose gods in *our* image—gods that suit our sinful desires. The one true God is an all-powerful God who loves us, redeems us from sin, and empowers us to worship Him alone.

BUILD YOUR OWN GOD (10 minutes)

Distribute copies of Student Page 30 and direct the students to the initial activity. After students mark their choices, ask, "Which characteristics do *not* describe our God?" (Leaves me alone, treats me as I deserve, does whatever I ask, made of gold) Invite responses to the student page questions. Then ask, "Would you like a god who leaves you alone when you are in trouble or who treats you as you deserve when you sin? How powerful is a god that you can boss around? Any god we could create would not be worthy of our worship. When we worship anything other than the triune God, we break the First Commandment."

A GOLDEN GOD (20 minutes)

Review Daniel 3:1–30 or have a student tell the story. In response to the questions, note:

In verses 16–18, the young men were certain God had the power to save them, even if He did not choose to do so. God did not have to prove Himself to them; they trusted Him even if they didn't understand His will.

In verses 28–29, the king was impressed by the faith of the young men and their willingness to suffer for it. He decreed that no one should say anything against their God.

ARE ALL GODS THE SAME? (20 minutes)

Discuss each statement. Then check the Bible passages. Emphasize that we do not want to ridicule the beliefs of others, but we do want to know and share the Bible's truth.

John 3:36—God does indeed love everyone, but we will not all end up in heaven. Those without faith in Jesus will experience God's wrath in hell.

John 12:48–50—Sorry, no. If you sincerely believe in brushing your teeth, you will not win salvation. Only believing the words of Jesus can give us the truth. Through them, the Holy Spirit works faith.

John 14:6—Because we are sinful people, we don't know the truth. We cannot find our own path to God or do anything to save ourselves. Jesus leads us to God. By His death and resurrection He has won eternal life for us.

Discuss the questions, making these points: Satan can't destroy Christianity, so he tries to dilute it. He wants us to believe all religions are the same so we won't share our faith with others. Encourage students to study God's Word so their faith is strong and they are ready to speak about Jesus and resist the temptation to worship the generic gods of the world.

CLOSING (5 minutes)

Sing or read together "Holy, Holy, Holy" (*LSB* 507, *LW* 168), stanzas 1 and 3. Then ask students to complete the phrase, "Hooray for God because He . . ." and share their completions as a closing prayer.

LESSON EXTENDERS

Discuss:

✝ "There are only two kinds of religion: in one (Christianity) we are saved solely by the work of God; in the other (all other religions) people try to save themselves."

✝ "Breaking any of the Ten Commandments involves breaking the First Commandment." How is this true?

IDOL NONSENSE

BUILD YOUR OWN GOD
If you could design and create your own god, which of the following characteristics would you give it?

- ☐ Leaves me alone
- ☐ Loving
- ☐ Forgiving
- ☐ Treats me as I deserve
- ☐ All-knowing
- ☐ Does whatever I ask
- ☐ Keeps promises
- ☐ Powerful
- ☐ Lives forever
- ☐ Not bound by space or time
- ☐ Generous
- ☐ Made of gold

If you could create the god you have described, would you want to worship it? Why or why not?

....
....
....

A GOLDEN GOD
King Nebuchadnezzar made his own god. He demanded that the entire society bow down and worship the ninety-foot-tall golden image or be thrown into a blazing furnace. Shadrach, Meshach, and Abednego refused. Read **Daniel 3:16–18**: How did these men show their faith?

....

The men were thrown into a fiery furnace, but God protected them, and they were unharmed. Read **Daniel 3:28–29** to discover how the king responded to the faith of these men.

....
....

ARE ALL GODS THE SAME?
There are many religions in the world today, chiefly because people have created their own images of god instead of relying on the truth found in the Bible. In today's society we are encouraged to worship a generic god who doesn't offend anyone. Read each statement below and look up the Bible passage that goes with it to discover whether the statement is true.

"God loves everyone so we will all end up in the same place anyway." **John 3:36**

"It doesn't matter what you believe, as long as you are sincere." **John 12:48–50**

"Everyone needs to find their own truth, their own path to God." **John 14:6**

Why might Satan want to convince us that one religion is as good as the next? How can you share the truth of God's Word with those who believe this?

....
....
....

STUDENT PAGE 30

Created in Christ © 2006 Concordia Publishing House. Reproduced by permission.

31. Daily Witnessing

Daniel 6:1–28

Lesson Focus

By the Spirit's guidance, faithful people trust and serve God, giving daily witness of God's goodness to those outside the faith.

TODAY'S QUOTE (15 minutes)

Distribute copies of Student Page 31. Ask students what is true about each of the quotes. Why might each of the quotes make us uncomfortable? On a scale of 1 to 10, have youths individually rank their Christian witness. Ask who they admire for their Christian witness and why.

GETTING INTO SCRIPTURE (15 minutes)

Read Daniel 6:1–28, answering questions on the student page and discussing the content of the story. Possible answers include the following: Daniel is appointed over all the kingdom. Some become jealous. Others find no fault with Daniel. Conspiracy (a clique) forms. Peers try to get Daniel into trouble. The king respects Daniel and wants to know more about his God. Daniel's life is put on the line for faith. Daniel is spared by God's grace, and his witness is strengthened. Students' personal answers will vary for the second set of responses.

GOING DEEPER (12 minutes)

Note the following while discussing the questions from the student page: The king is ready to make Daniel second-in-command due to Daniel's qualities and spirit. Daniel's actions reveal how he values the relationship with his God and how his devotion doesn't change even with threats of personal danger. Daniel's actions aren't arrogant or "holier than thou." According to verses 16 and 20, the king has apparently become impressed by Daniel's devotion and service to his God. Darius wants Daniel's God to rescue him from the possible harm that Darius has sentenced. It is not Daniel's innocence that saves him but God's grace, which brings about his protection from the lions (verse 22). Even though Daniel's witness impresses King Darius, Darius still doesn't understand much about God's love, continuing to do many things by force. He chooses to make rash decisions by punishing Daniel's accusers and issues a decree that all must fear the God of Daniel (verse 26). Daniel still needs to do much daily witnessing through loving words and deeds.

As justified children of God, we can reflect that through sanctified living. God can bring this about just as he brought about Daniel's willingness to risk his life.

CLOSING (3 minutes)

Read Psalm 46:10a. Like Daniel in our text, we can daily take time to quiet our lives by focusing on the blessings God gives. Close with the following prayer: "Lord Jesus, we fill our schedules and crowd You out. In the midst of busy days, give us a sense of peace. Guide us toward a rhythm of work and rest. Renew our weary spirits to be aligned with Your Spirit so that we witness to Your love. Amen."

LESSON EXTENDERS

✝ "I don't care how much you know until I know how much you care." Share examples from life that illustrate the truth behind this statement.

Daily Witnessing

TODAY'S QUOTE

"God does not comfort us to make us comfortable but to make us comforters."
(Anonymous)

"Always preach the Gospel. If necessary, use words."
(St. Francis of Assisi)

My ability to make use of most witness opportunities

low   1   2   3   4   5   6   7   8   9   10   high

My witness effectiveness

low   1   2   3   4   5   6   7   8   9   10   high

GETTING INTO SCRIPTURE

According to **Daniel 6**, what happens (both good and bad) due to Daniel's work performance?

1.
2.
3.
4.

What might happen (good and bad) if I have the Spirit of Christ leading me throughout my day?

1.
2.
3.
4.

GOING DEEPER

Why would the king be so distressed about arresting Daniel and so willing to try to save him from harm (**verses 14–20**)?

What is Daniel willing to risk?

What am I willing to risk?

32. Second Chances

Jonah 1:1–4:11

Lesson Focus

God demonstrates His love by providing second chances to sinful people through His Son, Jesus Christ.

OPENING (5 minutes)

Write "Delayed obedience is disobedience" on the board. Begin your study by asking the students to write whether they agree or disagree with the statement on a note card or scrap of paper. Discuss whether obedience can be subject to convenient timing, circumstances, or one's opinion of the request. (Perhaps it can in some arenas of life, but God's Law allows no such conditional obedience.)

WARM-UP QUESTIONS (10 minutes)

Distribute copies of Student Page 32 and allow the students to complete the three "Warm-up Questions." Then discuss the following questions.

1. "When you were last asked to do something you didn't want to do, what happened?" (Answers will vary.)

2. "What do you do when God asks things that you don't want to do?" (Some people rationalize their disobedience. Some may "just do the best they can." Some may obey, but whine. Some may blatantly sin.)

3. "Does God ever ask more of you than you can do? Explain." (We may certainly *feel* overwhelmed, but God's promise is to never *overload* us. See Isaiah 42:3a.)

THE STORY OF JONAH (20 minutes)

Invite the students to scan the four chapters of Jonah and respond to the questions in the chart on the student page. Invite comments about new insights they may have. Then review by saying, "Jonah's situation was a lot like ours. He had been told by God to warn people he really didn't like about God's wrath. Because he didn't agree with what God told him to do, he tried to run away from God. Eventually, Jonah obeyed and preached God's word in Nineveh. The city repented and was saved. God gave Jonah and the city a second chance. God gives us second chances as well."

APPLICATION (15 minutes)

Invite the students to mark the scale on the student page. Then say, "God loves us and wants to help us. His Son paid the penalty for our disobedience. Through Jesus, we receive the Holy Spirit, new life, and both the desire and the ability to obey God. Everyday, God gives us second chances, just as He did with Jonah." Discuss:

"Who among your friends has hurt you, has said they are sorry, and needs your forgiveness and a second chance?"

"Whom among your friends have you hurt? From whom do you need to ask forgiveness and a second chance?"

"In what ways could we extend the second chance of God's grace to others in our community?"

CLOSING (5 minutes)

Lead the students in this prayer: "Dear Lord, You love us so much that You gave us a second chance to live forever through Your Son, Jesus. Help us give others second chances. Especially help us share with them the Good News of Your love and forgiveness. In Jesus' name. Amen."

LESSON EXTENDERS

✞ How many of the Bible's "second chances" can your students remember? (Adam and Eve, Genesis 3; the whole world, Genesis 9; Moses, Exodus 3; etc.)

✞ Outline a worship service on "Second Chances," choosing Scripture readings and songs and writing litanies for confession and prayer.

Second Chances

WARM-UP QUESTIONS

Answer the following questions by circling the response that best describes you.

1. When someone asks me to do something, I . . .

(a) say I'd love to!   (b) put it off.   (c) get someone else to do it.

2. When I don't want to do what I'm asked, I . . .

(a) do it anyway.   (b) put it off.   (c) run to Spain.

3. When I get caught avoiding people or tasks, I . . .

(a) apologize.   (b) blame others.   (c) pout.

THE STORY OF JONAH

Review **Jonah 1:1–4:11**, then fill in the chart below as honestly as possible. (You will not be required to share your answers.)

What was Jonah told to do?	
Why didn't he do it?	
What happened when he didn't obey at first?	
What happened when he finally did obey?	
What would you have done if you had been Jonah? Why?	

APPLICATION

Put an X on a spot on the scale below to represent where you are now. Next, place an O on a spot to indicate where you want to be in two weeks.

When God speaks I . . .

obey   put Him on hold   say no   listen   ignore the call

Created in Christ © 2006 Concordia Publishing House. Reproduced by permission.

33. GOD'S TIMING

Luke 1:5–25

Lesson Focus

God is faithful in carrying out His Word, even when we are not patient but want immediate answers.

TIME-SAVERS (5 minutes)

Distribute copies of Student Page 33. Ask students why someone might define Americans like the statement on the student page. Ask for examples of how this definition might be true. Be prepared to list examples if the students do not suggest any.

CHOICES (15 minutes)

Read Luke 1:5–25 and discuss the choices on the student page. According to today's values, would Zechariah and Elizabeth be entitled to be impatient and take control of their hopes and dreams for a child?

WAITING GAME (10 minutes)

Discuss what Elizabeth and Zechariah may have done while trying to have a child. Yes, this includes having sexual intercourse, but what else might they have done? For example, other couples from the Bible had a child by means of a servant. Other possibilities include praying, waiting, being impatient, being angry, adopting a child, continuing with their life by being thankful for what they have, and so forth.

PONDERING (15 minutes)

Have students check out Romans 11:33–36. God's ways and His timing are not necessarily our ways or according to our timing. Our American culture emphasizes that we have a right to what we want and we deserve to have it immediately (instant gratification, not biblical). We are not accustomed to waiting very long for anything because we are neither taught nor encouraged to wait. Today's technology is aimed at bringing about rapid communication and faster distribution of products. Yet patience is included in the fruit of the Spirit (Galatians 5:22). Also check out Philippians 4:6: "Do not be anxious about anything." Compare these passages to the messages of commercials and advertisements. God is always faithful and patient with us even though we want immediate answers and proofs from Him. God gives us His Spirit to assist us in developing the patience that we need.

CLOSING (5 minutes)

Perhaps we are like the person whose prayer was, "God, give me patience, and give it to me NOW!" Lead the students in prayer that God would help each person develop the gift of patience as we wait on His perfect timing. Be sure to include any specific prayer concerns that students may mention.

LESSON EXTENDERS

✝ Discuss ways that we can be more patient with others, whether as individuals or collectively as groups.

GOD'S TIMING

TIME-SAVERS

Americans: "People with more timesaving devices yet less time than anybody else in the world." Is this true? Why or why not?

....

....

CHOICES

| Having an angel speak to you | Which would be more **surprising**? | Being told that you will have a child when you are beyond childbearing age |

| Being told to get ready to meet God | Which would be more **surprising**? | Being told you are to help people get ready to meet God |

| Being told to get ready for being in God's presence | Which would be more **frightening**? | Being asked to be God's presence to others |

| Being asked to be a speaker for God | Which would be more **frightening**? | Discovering that you are unable to speak |

| Having a spiritual vision | Which would make you more **comfortable**? | Hearing someone talk about a spiritual vision they had |

WAITING GAME

What do you think Elizabeth and Zechariah may have done while trying to have a child?

....
....
....
....
....
....

PONDERING

Read **Romans 11:33–36**; **Galatians 5:22**; and **Philippians 4:6**.

What common thread can you draw from these verses?

....
....
....

How does this compare with our "have it your way" mentality?

....
....
....

Created in Christ © 2006 Concordia Publishing House. Reproduced by permission.

34. Chosen

Luke 1:26–55

Lesson Focus

Just as God chose Mary, He chooses us and gives us what we need.

CHOSEN? (10 minutes)

Distribute copies of Student Page 34. Read or ask someone to read the list of choices, then allow students to respond. Don't dwell on any particular task. Expect mixed and varied reactions.

Continue by reading and discussing the questions. What factors influenced students' reactions?

CHOSEN! (20 minutes)

Read the selected verses from Luke. Discuss the questions with the whole class. Elizabeth provided her relative Mary a place to go and the emotional support Mary needed. Even though there was a scandal, God directly encouraged Joseph to support Mary.

Read the texts from 2 Thessalonians and Isaiah. Allow time for students to answer and discuss questions. God's Holy Spirit chose us from the beginning, called us through the Gospel, sanctifies us, and helps us believe in the truth. God gave us the Bible and empowers people to teach it to us. God is with us, so we don't have to be afraid or worried. He will strengthen, help, and support us.

NOW WHAT? (15 minutes)

Read the questions and give students time to respond. Ask students to share what they are comfortable with. Encourage students by pointing out positive opportunities, talents, and available help.

CLOSING (5 minutes)

Invite students to think of some task or challenge they are currently facing and some help God has given them to deal with it. Let them pray individually, in pairs, or in a group using this model: "Dear God, thank You for giving me _____ to help me deal with _____."

Then close the prayer by asking, "God, please help us see Your love and guidance during the coming week. Thank You for being there for us. Amen."

LESSON EXTENDERS

✝ Read Luke 1:46–55. Mary is singing to God. What is she telling Him? As Christians who trust in God for forgiveness and eternal life, we are also considered descendants of Abraham. We can thank God for His goodness to us. If you could sing or write a song of praise, what might you say?

✝ Pass out an envelope for each student to address with his or her name. Provide students with enough small pieces of paper so they have a piece for every other student in the class. Have students write a note or phrase to each member of the class describing a characteristic or talent God has given him or her. Collect the envelopes and notes. Review notes outside of class to remove any that are inappropriate. The following week return the envelopes to each student with the affirmations from their fellow class members.

Chosen

CHOSEN?

Which of these would you like to be chosen for, and which would you rather not?

- ____ Be selected to write a story for a group project
- ____ Be chosen captain of the school team
- ____ Work as equipment manager for the school team
- ____ Clean up after an art project
- ____ Paint a mural on a wall
- ____ Take your grandmother shopping
- ____ Wear a "kick me" sign on your back
- ____ Go to Disney World
- ____ Go on a trip with your elderly neighbor to carry his/her oxygen
- ____ Take the dog for a walk
- ____ Clean up the dog's area while he is gone

Why do you like to be chosen for some things, but prefer not to be chosen for others?

Does the person choosing influence how you react?

Would your answer change if you could choose someone to help you?

CHOSEN!

Read **Luke 1:26–45**.

Who chose Mary? For what purpose was Mary chosen?

Was this part of Mary's plan? What plan was it part of?

What help did God provide for Mary?

Read **2 Thessalonians 2:13–17** and **Isaiah 41:10**.

Who chose each of us?

What has He done to help us?

What help does He continue to offer?

NOW WHAT?

What else has God chosen you for?

How is He offering to help you?

STUDENT PAGE 34

Created in Christ © 2006 Concordia Publishing House. Reproduced by permission.

35. Sticks and Stones

Luke 1:57–80

Lesson Focus

Throughout Scripture, names have great significance. The most important name, however, is that of Christ Jesus, our Lord and Savior.

STICKS AND STONES MAY BREAK MY BONES
(10 minutes)

Distribute copies of Student Page 35. Lead students through the sticks and stones opening section. Encourage students to talk about the positive and negative effects names can have on people. When they have finished sharing, say something like, "Names, despite what the old saying says, *can* hurt or encourage us. Names in the Bible were very important in describing the significance of people, places, and events. In today's lesson we're going to look at how a name can powerfully affect our lives."

WHAT'S IN A NAME?
(10 minutes)

Ask your class to turn to Luke 1:57–80. Walk them through these verses, and answer the questions together as a group. Answers: People expected a child to have the same name as his father—like father, like son! A person's name suggested something about his life's purpose. John means "the Lord has been gracious"; "favor of God"; or "God's gift." John announced the coming of God's kingdom and salvation for the world. Students may have a variety of ideas about how John's parents treated him. John probably understood that God had a very special purpose in mind for him. Jesus means "Savior." At the name of Jesus: Acts 2:38—forgiveness of sins; Acts 4:10—healing; Acts 16:18—casting out demons; Philippians 2:10—every knee bows before Him.

An Old Name
(10 minutes)

In the days of the early church, "fish" was not simply the name of a creature, but a profession of faith. In the times of persecution, one could be imprisoned or killed simply for being known as a follower of Jesus. To secretly find other believers, early Christians would draw a curved line in the sand. Another believer would then draw an additional curved line that would make the outline of a fish. The word *fish* in Greek is *ICHTHUS*, or $IX\Theta Y\Sigma$. It is an acrostic, with each Greek letter representing one word of a simple creed: I—Jesus; X—Christ; Θ—God's; Y—Son; Σ—Savior. The fish became a symbol of the Christian faith.

Invite students to write the words of the acrostic below the fish. Ask your class, "What differences are there in these names for God? Why do you think all are important for this 'creed'?" Conclude this section by saying something like, "The *ichthus* is a simple reminder of the power that is in a name—not the name of a creature, but the name of the One who has redeemed all creation, Jesus Christ. And the power that is in His name is given to us by grace through faith. It is the name given to us at our Baptism."

A NEW NAME (15 minutes)

Explain that because of Jesus' death and resurrection, we, as Christians, have His name and His power at work in our lives. Direct your class to the student page directions. Ask them to pick a name from the ones listed on the page, or another one they might think of based on a Bible passage, that describes what God has done for us in Christ. Encourage students to share which word they picked and why it is meaningful to them at this particular time. Close your time together by having students pray for each other.

Sticks and Stones

STICKS AND STONES MAY BREAK MY BONES

Hero   Jerk   Tease   Savior   Wimp
Stud   Chicken   Hunk   Christian   Player

Take a look at the names found on this page. Share what kind of people you think are represented by them.

....

What names (these or others) have you been called?

....

How have they affected you?

....

WHAT'S IN A NAME?

What were people expecting Elizabeth and Zechariah to name their son and why (**Luke 1:59–61**)?

....

What does **Luke 1:66** tell you about the power of a name?

....

What does the name *John* mean?

....

How is the meaning of John's name reflected in who he was and what his purpose was?

....

How do you think **Luke 1:76** affected the way John's parents viewed and raised him? How do you think it affected John's view of himself?

....

What does the name *Jesus* mean (**Matthew 1:21**)?

....

In the following passages, what power do you see in the name of Jesus?

Acts 2:38

....

Acts 4:10

....

Acts 16:18

....

Philippians 2:10

....

AN OLD NAME

A NEW NAME

Because of the One named Jesus, you and I have been given a new name: forgiven and loved child of God. Look at the names below that describe benefits of your new identity in Christ. Circle the one that has special meaning in your life right now.

Chosen (**John 15:16**)

Forgiven (**1 John 2:12**)

Free (**John 8:36**)

Cleansed (**Titus 3:5–8**)

Alive (**Ephesians 2:4–5**)

Redeemed (**Isaiah 44:22**)

Valued by God (**Matthew 6:26**)

New creation (**2 Corinthians 5:17**)

Child of God (**1 John 3:1**)

STUDENT PAGE 35

Created in Christ © 2006 Concordia Publishing House. Reproduced by permission.

36. He's Got a Plan

Matthew 1:18–25; Isaiah 7:10–14

Lesson Focus

Students will see how the power of God, evident in His salvation plan through the incarnation, also helps us face difficult issues.

SAY WHAT? (10 minutes)

Distribute copies of Student Page 36. Have a student volunteer read Matthew 1:18–19. Have students complete one of the two statements on the student page. Ask a few students to share their statements.

WHAT'S GOING ON? (10 minutes)

Joseph and Mary found themselves in a difficult situation. Mary's news was hard to understand and Joseph had to decide whether to believe her or not. Today's lesson helps us cope with difficult issues in our own lives.

On the student page, have students list one or more difficult situations they or a friend may be facing right now. You may want to share a difficult situation you have faced in your own life.

Ask students to think about how complicated Mary and Joseph's lives may have become when she became pregnant by the Holy Spirit.

GOD HAS A PLAN (20 minutes)

Have students work together in small groups to create an outline of Matthew 1:18–25 and Isaiah 7:10–14 using the references on the student page. Summarize the events of Isaiah 7:1–9 to provide students with the context of the crisis found there. Below is a suggested format and outline:

Matthew 1:18–25	Isaiah 7:10–14
vv. 18–19 Crisis: Mary pregnant	**vv. 10–11** Crisis: Test of faith
v. 20 Test of faith and choice: Obey or disobey	**v. 12** Choice: Obey or disobey
vv. 21–23 God's plan	**v. 13** Rebuke for disobedience
vv. 24–25 Joseph's obedience	**v. 14** God's plan

Ask students to search for the parallels between the Gospel messages in the two texts. God has a plan to save His people. Neither Ahaz nor Joseph could see into the future. Both trusted in God's plan.

A CLOSER LOOK (10 minutes)

Have students look back at the difficult situation they listed earlier. Life is complicated, and we, like Ahaz and Joseph, face difficult situations. Sometimes we are faithful (like Joseph) and other times we are unfaithful (like Ahaz).

Have students read 2 Timothy 2:11–13. Help them answer the question on the student page. Even when we are unfaithful to our calling as Christians, God remains faithful.

Have students answer the last question on the student page and discuss.

CLOSING (5 minutes)

Lead students in a prayer asking God to help them remain faithful in the face of difficult times now and in the future.

LESSON EXTENDERS

✞ Your students may be facing a serious crisis right now. Extend an invitation to the students to come and talk to you confidentially. Alternatively, refer them to the pastor or another trusted adult.

✞ Help students reflect on a possible life/faith crisis that might arise in the future. Thinking now about how they might respond then can help students cope with issues in the future. Invite students to brainstorm appropriate ways to respond.

He's Got a Plan

SAY WHAT?

Read **Matthew 1:18–19**. Put yourself in the role of Mary or Joseph and complete one of the following statements.

Mary: Joseph, I have to tell you . . .

....

Joseph: Mary, . . .

....

WHAT'S GOING ON?

Take a moment and list one or more difficult situations you or a friend may be facing right now.

....

....

GOD HAS A PLAN

Summarize each verse to form an outline of the events in Matthew and Isaiah.

Matthew 1:18–25	**Isaiah 7:10–14**
vv. 18–19	vv. 10–11
v. 20	v. 12
vv. 21–23	v. 13
vv. 24–25	v. 14

What parallels do you see between the two texts?

....

What's the Gospel/power in the two texts?

....

A CLOSER LOOK

Read **2 Timothy 2:11–13**. What is the good news in this text?

How does this text, along with the other Scriptures for today, apply to the situation you listed above in "What's Going On?"

....

....

....

....

....

....

....

....

STUDENT PAGE 36

37. The Young and the Faithful

Luke 2:40–52

Lesson Focus

In this story of Jesus as a preteen, students will understand that God grants and strengthens the faith of young people and, through the righteousness of Jesus, He forgives their rebellious actions toward their parents.

Godly Growth (20 minutes)

Distribute copies of Student Page 37. Assign one of the passages to each student or group. After each group shares its findings, lead these discussion questions: Is anyone too young for God to work in his or her life? Are you wiser about the things of God today than you were last year? five years ago? If so, why do you believe you are wiser?

The Perfect Youth (15 minutes)

Ask a volunteer to read aloud the Luke passage. Then, as a group, work through the questions. Lead students to understand these points:

Joseph and Mary fulfill Jewish law by going to Jerusalem for the Passover Feast. This annual trip often became a kind of family vacation with friends, food, and in this case a "coming of age" time for Jesus. At age 12 Jesus understands Himself as God's Son and a young man with a human family. This passage shows that it was a challenge for the whole family to figure out what it all meant. Some Bible scholars believe that this is the first time Jesus acknowledges His understanding of who He is to other persons. His parents may have been surprised by His actions. Jesus is not angry with nor is He chastising His parents nor is He being a flippant teenager. All of these actions would be sinful; they would break the Fourth Commandment. He may have simply lost track of time, which can occur without being a sin.

Christ's Perfection—Our Righteousness (10 minutes)

Help students understand Jesus' obedience to His earthly parents as part of "being about His heavenly Father's business." Read Luther's explanation of the Fourth Commandment from the Small Catechism, and have students complete the scale. Ask volunteers to share. Have students read Hebrews 2:17 for themselves and be ready to share their answers. Because Jesus was like us in every way except without sin, He now also understands our relationship with our parents.

Closing (5 minutes)

Speak the following prayer: "Dear heavenly Father, we know that You desire for each of us to grow in wisdom, stature, and favor with You and with others. Thank You that through our Baptism You gave us Your Spirit and enable us to grow in faith. As we grow up and become responsible adults, help us honor, serve, and obey our parents—to love and cherish them. When we fail to live out our faith in You, we are most thankful for Jesus who, because He lived a perfect life, even as a teenager, makes forgiveness of our sins possible. In His name we pray. Amen."

Lesson Extenders

✦ Use a Bible dictionary to learn more about the Passover Feast and customs. Especially note how Jesus fulfills the Passover Feast through His death and resurrection during the Passover season.

✦ Read the full section regarding the Fourth Commandment in the explanation section of Luther's Small Catechism (questions 48–51).

THE YOUNG AND THE FAITHFUL

GODLY GROWTH

Read the passages below and answer the three questions for each:

Who is the passage about?

About how old is this person?

What is the key idea of the passage?

1 Timothy 4:12

....

....

1 Samuel 2:26

....

....

Luke 1:80

....

....

Luke 2:40

....

....

Luke 2:52

....

....

THE PERFECT YOUTH

Read **Luke 2:40–52**.

Compare verses **41–42** with **Deuteronomy 16:1, 5–6**. Describe what this "family vacation" may have been like for Jesus and His family.

Reread **verses 48–49**; note who Mary says Jesus' father is and who Jesus refers to as His Father. What does this indicate about Jesus' understanding of Himself?

How would you describe the actions of Mary and Joseph in this story?

....

....

How would you describe Jesus' actions in this story?

....

....

CHRIST'S PERFECTION—OUR RIGHTEOUSNESS

What words in this account tell you about Jesus' obedience to His earthly parents as well as to His heavenly Father?

Place an *X* on a number on the scale to show how well Jesus fulfilled the Fourth Commandment, and circle how well you fulfill it:

(rebel against it)   1   2   3   4   5   6   7   8   9   10   (fulfill it perfectly)

According to **Hebrews 2:17**, how are Jesus' teenage years a part of God's grace to you?

....

Created in Christ © 2006 Concordia Publishing House. Reproduced by permission.

38. New Beginnings

Matthew 3:13–17

Lesson Focus

Students will see Christ begin His ministry and see their calling by God to share His Love.

BEFORE THE STUDY BEGINS

Use a squirt gun to welcome students into the room. This can remind students of the daily impact of their Baptism. Mention that today's study will be about new beginnings in faith and that in their Baptism God gave them a new life.

TIME FOR THE KICKOFF (5 minutes)

Hand out copies of Student Page 38. Have students answer the four questions in the opening activity. Give them hints, if necessary. (The ball drop, champagne bottle broken on the bow, the cutting of the ribbon, and a wedding ceremony) Say, "We have all kinds of kickoff events for various events in our life. What are some others you can think of?" Allow students to respond.

WE'RE JUST GETTING STARTED (20 minutes)

Ask the students to continue reading on the student page. Encourage responses to the questions. Be prepared with a personal story to get the discussion started. You may want to talk about your wedding, confirmation, or Baptism. Note that beginnings are a time of excitement and hopefulness. As with a new year, you have a chance to start over again by making resolutions to do things differently. Some beginnings in church include Baptisms, confirmations, weddings, commissionings, and ordinations. Talk about what each of these ceremonies begins. Take a look at another beginning in Matthew 3:13–17.

Read the passage and discuss the four questions. Possible answers:

Jesus said He was baptized "to fulfill all righteousness"—He was consecrated by God to set an example to demonstrate His full humanity (yet without sin) and His role as our substitute, as well as to allow John to publicly identify Him as the Messiah and announce the beginning of His public ministry.

Our Baptism was done at Christ's command for the forgiveness of sin and, in many cases, as the beginning of faith.

Father: In the voice from heaven; Son: Jesus; Holy Spirit: as a dove.

God is present at each Baptism, God applies His redemptive work to the baptized, the Spirit enters the heart, forgiveness of sins through Jesus is present.

Explore another beginning in the early church recorded in Acts 2:1–4. Allow time to discuss the four questions. Possible answers:

The day of Pentecost, a Jewish holiday when many Jews returned to Jerusalem.

Similarities: People entered the kingdom of God by water and the Spirit, as the Word was connected with the water. Differences: Done to others, not Jesus—but in Jesus' name.

At our Baptism God forgives our sins, gives us new life, and makes us His child. This beginning continues throughout our life.

KEEPING IT FRESH (10 minutes)

Read the paragraph from the student page. Discuss the questions and be prepared to give your own answers. Point out that Martin Luther said we are to renew our Baptism daily. You may wish to remind yourself of that every day in the shower. Remind students that God forgives and "will remember [our] sins no more" (Jeremiah 31:34). The past is gone and forgiven forever. We have a new life every day in Christ. The fresh, clean feeling of a morning shower can remind you of the new perspective you have as God's forgiven child.

CLOSING (5 minutes)

Invite students to pair up and pray with each other, asking God to refresh their Spirit and keep things new in their faith each day. Invite students to remember their Baptism each day of the coming week in the shower as they are cleansed by water.

New Beginnings

TIME FOR THE KICKOFF

What symbolizes the beginning of each of these events?

A New Year in New York's Times Square _____

The launching of a new ship _____

The grand opening of a new building _____

A marriage _____

WE'RE JUST GETTING STARTED

What big opening ceremonies or beginnings have you witnessed or been a part of?

What, if anything, made them special?

What new beginnings are celebrated at our church?

Read **Matthew 3:13–17**.
This Baptism marked the beginning of Jesus' ministry. Why do you think Jesus was baptized?

How is Jesus' Baptism different from your own?

How was each person of the Trinity (Father, Son, and Holy Spirit) present at Jesus' Baptism?

What makes every Baptism special?

Read **Acts 2:1–4**.
What event does this passage describe?

What are the similarities to and differences from Jesus' Baptism?

When did we receive the Holy Spirit?

How does God make our Baptism a new beginning?

KEEPING IT FRESH

We celebrate beginnings in special ways, but the newness often wears off. Years pass by and new ones come, ships get old and worn, buildings crumble and fall, and all marriages end, either by death or divorce. But God's love in Baptism will never fade away.

So how does faith stay vibrant?

How does the newness of Baptism stay fresh?

How does God's forgiveness keep things new?

God is at work sustaining and nurturing our faith.

How is Baptism like . . .

a scrapbook?

a washing machine?

a family tree?

STUDENT PAGE 38

Created in Christ © 2006 Concordia Publishing House. Reproduced by permission.

39. Jesus: The Life of the Party?

John 2:1–11

Lesson Focus

Often our image of Jesus is of someone on a serious mission. This session reminds us that Jesus also took time to enjoy the common celebrations of life. In the same way, Jesus can bring joy beyond imagination into our daily lives.

OPENING (5 minutes)

Gather different pictures of Jesus from around your church or home. Ask students to identify the difference in how Jesus is depicted in each picture. Invite students to share how they most often picture Jesus and where that image came from.

PICTURE THIS (10 minutes)

Distribute copies of Student Page 39. Give students a moment to read the options and select one or more of them. Discuss the reasons for their choices. Challenge them to think of biblical situations similar to those listed.

Say, "We usually don't think of Jesus dancing the night away at a wedding. We usually picture Him being on a serious mission. Today's lesson will remind us that our Savior also took time to celebrate and bring joy to our lives."

JESUS CELEBRATES (15 minutes)

Ask a volunteer to read aloud John 2:1–11. Use the questions on the student page to review the story. Explain that a wedding feast in Jesus' day was a big occasion, lasting up to a week. Running out of wine at the feast would have been a major humiliation. Jesus' miracle spared this family a good deal of embarrassment. Discuss why Jesus chose this as His first miracle and what it says about Him. How does this miracle show Jesus' care for the ordinary things in our lives?

Say, "Jesus' first miracle may not have been spectacular. But through it, Jesus reminds us that He is part of our daily lives. If He cares for the everyday things, how much more does He care for the important things?"

MY CUP OVERFLOWS! (15 minutes)

Ask the students to note the water jars Jesus used for this miracle. These jars were used for the ceremonial purification of hands, which was an obligation of the Jews. Point out that Jesus turned something that was Law into grace! Jesus took a reminder of the Law and turned it into an example of His overflowing love for us.

Have students identify other accounts of God's overflowing goodness. Possible answers might include manna in the wilderness (Exodus 16), the feeding of the five thousand (John 6:5–13), or the miraculous catch of fish (John 21:1–14).

Read the verses listed on the student page and discuss how they show the abundance of God's grace for us.

CLOSING (5 minutes)

Provide a small reminder of Jesus' presence, such as a cross sticker, for students to place somewhere they see daily. Encourage this as a reminder of Jesus in their everyday lives. Invite the class to speak the words of Ephesians 3:20–21 together as a closing benediction.

LESSON EXTENDERS

- Share a specific time in your life when you feel that God provided more than you asked. Encourage students to do the same. Challenge students to ask their family members to share such a time.

- Have students create an invitation for Jesus to attend an upcoming event to remind us that He is always present.

Jesus: The Life of the Party?

PICTURE THIS

If Jesus were on earth today, where would you picture Him being?

- ☐ Preaching at a large service
- ☐ Playing with children on the playground
- ☐ Leading a Bible class at our church
- ☐ Helping serve a meal at homeless shelter
- ☐ Taking time alone to pray in a peaceful spot like a park or garden
- ☐ Having dinner at your home
- ☐ Dancing the night away at your cousin's wedding
- ☐ Healing patients at a local hospital
- ☐ Stopping a funeral to comfort the family and raise the dead loved one

JESUS CELEBRATES

Read **John 2:1–11**. Where was Jesus in this story?

....

What problem came up?

....

How did Jesus respond? What was the result?

....

This was Jesus' first miracle. Why do you think Jesus didn't choose something more dramatic, such as a healing, to make His "debut"? What does this miracle tell us about Jesus?

....

MY CUP OVERFLOWS!

Look back at the story. What does the text tell us about the water jars Jesus used in this miracle?

....

The six water jars mentioned in the story probably held 20–30 gallons each. That would mean that Jesus provided 120–180 gallons of wine for the wedding feast! This was certainly more than enough to meet the need. Can you think of other stories in which God provided "more than enough"?

Read about God's overflowing goodness in the following verses:

Psalm 23

....

Romans 15:13

....

Ephesians 3:17–21

....

Now to Him who is able to do immeasurably more than all we ask or imagine, according to His power that is at work within us, to Him be glory in the church and in Christ Jesus throughout all generations, for ever and ever! Amen. **(Ephesians 3:20–21)**

STUDENT PAGE 39

Created in Christ © 2006 Concordia Publishing House. Scripture: NIV®. Reproduced by permission.

40. Doing What Disciples Do

Mark 1:14–20

Lesson Focus

God calls us to be His disciples, communicates His mission through His Word, and promises to support our service.

DISCIPLES DO LEARNING (10 minutes)

Distribute copies of Student Page 40. Challenge the students to mark the value assessment. Ask, "Which area of learning influences your Christian discipleship the most?"

Have the students read Mark 1:14–20 and ponder the questions on the student page. (1) The first disciples changed as they saw their hopes for the Messiah fulfilled in Jesus and became Jesus-centered, kingdom people, seeking to save the lost. (2) In Christ, we too are changed, called to leave the darkness of sin and live in the light of Christ. (3) For Jesus' first disciples, and for us, these changes result from God working in our lives through the Gospel.

DISCIPLES DO FOLLOWING (10 minutes)

Say, "Luke 14:25–33 shows the essence of discipleship—dropping everything and following Jesus—making Him our highest priority." Discuss the questions. (1) Being a disciple could literally cost everything. Remind the students of this important Gospel message: Jesus paid the cost for our discipleship—His own life. Without the influence of His love, we would be unwilling and unable to follow Him. (2) Jesus' command to "hate" our family is hard to hear. Jesus is saying that we must love Him even more than our family. For disciples, He is number 1; number 2 is way down the list.

DISCIPLES DO HAVE A MISSION (15 minutes)

Talk about the work given to disciples and to us as followers today. *Mark 6:7–13*—Jesus sends His followers out to preach the Gospel and heal the sick. As His disciples today, we are to reflect Jesus' light and bring His healing Gospel to our schools, friends, and whole community. *Luke 9:13–17*—Jesus challenged His disciples to do what seemed impossible. As disciples today, we are also called to do impossibly difficult things—standing up for our faith, defending a weaker person, challenging the behavior of friends who don't follow Jesus. It is God who works through us in these things, His power that sustains us. *Matthew 28:18–20*—Jesus sends His disciples—then and now—to go into the world and lead others to follow Him.

DISCIPLES DO HAVE JESUS' PROMISES (10 minutes)

Perhaps the best part of following Jesus is knowing He is with us as we pick up our cross and follow. These three promises will keep young disciples strong in Jesus. *Matthew 28:20b*—Jesus will never leave His disciples. His gracious presence means forgiveness and peace even when we fail. *John 21:15–19*—Jesus is willing to push a disciple to follow fully, but, even more important, He forgives and renews. *Mark 1:17*—Jesus promises us a compelling purpose to our lives, sharing Him with others.

CLOSING (5 MINUTES)

Lead the students in a prayer. Encourage and allow time for the students to pray aloud for immediate needs—their own and those of their friends.

LESSON EXTENDERS

✟ Display the following list for the students, asking them to consider what they would be willing to give up to follow Jesus: material things, money, how I spend my time, my friends, my family, my country, my life. Where will Jesus' disciples draw the line?

✟ Have the students think of a time they have paid a price for following Jesus.

Doing What Disciples Do

WHAT DOES IT MEAN TO BE A DISCIPLE?

You have been called in Baptism to be Jesus' follower. What does it mean to follow Jesus and let other things drop in our lives?

What is it that disciples do?

DISCIPLES DO FOLLOWING

Jesus' first disciples dropped everything to follow Him. Read **Luke 14:25–33**.

1. According to these verses, what cost is there to following Jesus?

2. Does Jesus *overstate* what is necessary? What does He really mean?

DISCIPLES DO LEARNING

Rate these sources of learning from 1–10 (1 being most important, 10 being least important).

___ School ___ Friends ___ Family ___ Teachers ___ Pastor
___ Television ___ Internet ___ Other adults ___ Books ___ Newspapers

Read **Mark 1:14–20**.

1. How do you think the values and lives of these fishermen changed when they followed Jesus?

2. How have your values changed as you follow Jesus? What further changes do you expect?

3. How do these changes take place?

DISCIPLES DO HAVE A MISSION

Disciples are busy people. They have been called to follow Jesus and been set free to do so with love. Read the following verses and consider your mission as a disciple.

	The First Disciples' Mission	**My Mission**
Mark 6:7–13		
Luke 9:13–17		
Matthew 28:18–20		

DISCIPLES DO HAVE JESUS' PROMISES

Matthew 28:20b

John 21:15–19

Mark 1:17

STUDENT PAGE 40

41. OVERCOMING ADVERSITY

Mark 1:40–45

Lesson Focus

By the power of the Holy Spirit, students will see weaknesses as means through which salvation can be proclaimed and God glorified, whether for healing or for giving strength to endure adversity.

OPENING (5 minutes)

Distribute copies of Student Page 41. Read the opening paragraph. Point out that the media often portrays people as triumphing over adversity through their own effort. No credit is given to God, who alone sustains and heals believer and unbeliever alike.

WHAT'S THE ISSUE? (15 minutes)

Discuss the questions. Encourage students to share problems that they and their peers face today. Explore implications such as, "How might such a person feel? How will the person react to others? Why does the person suffering from acne retreat from other teens? How can we minister to such people?"

In Isaiah 43:1–2, God reminds us that He created us, redeems us, and knows us *by name*. We have a personal God who is concerned about our lives and who is always with us.

Romans 5:1–8 reveals God's great love for us. God knew all people would be sinners, yet He willingly gave His Son on a cross for us. This is how God proves His love for us—only in Christ!

Read the concluding paragraph of this section as a summary.

INTO THE WORD (20 minutes)

Read Mark 1:40–45 and discuss the questions, supplementing student responses with this information:

1. The man said: "You can make me clean." Since only God could heal leprosy at that time, the man must have believed Jesus to be God.
2. It was not because of this man's actions, personality, or even need. Jesus healed this leper because of the same love He has for each of us.
3. Answers may vary. Some might say that many people would then come to Jesus seeking cures, but not recognizing Him as the promised Savior. The man spread the news of his healing abroad.
4. God's glory is revealed because, by God's grace, Paul continues to love and serve God without healing. Whether through healing or through strengthening us to endure, God provides reason for His people to tell His story.

WHAT'S YOUR ISSUE? (10 minutes)

Discuss the first question. Some teens may be caught up in their problems and miss God's solution. Some may have weak faith. Some may be misled by others. See Matthew 11:28–29. Emphasize that there is no problem too small or too large to talk over with God.

CLOSING (5 minutes)

Use the final question on the student page to begin a time of silent prayer, then close with prayers of thanks and petitions for strength.

LESSON EXTENDERS

Discuss:

- Jesus didn't want the man healed of leprosy to tell others. Later He told His disciples to share His Good News with others. Why this change? (Only after His suffering and death on the cross of Calvary and His subsequent resurrection did Jesus fully and completely use His divine powers. Then He instructed His disciples to share that Good News with others freely.)
- Why aren't all prayers for healing and deliverance answered right away? (Sometimes God allows problems in our lives in order to teach us or, as the Scriptures say, to discipline us and strengthen our faith. [See Romans 5:3–4; Hebrews 12:4–11.])

OVERCOMING ADVERSITY

A tennis professional, born with four deformed limbs, describes himself as *inconvenienced* rather than handicapped. A high school athlete, paralyzed from the waist down at age 17, becomes a wheelchair athletic champion. A young woman with multiple sclerosis describes her MS as the gift that slowed her down to appreciate life. A prominent movie star, paralyzed below the neck in a horse-jumping fall, became an advocate for health care reform. For these and thousands of others, adversity is not a dead end.

WHAT'S THE ISSUE?

What adversities or physical problems do you or your friends face right now that destroy self-confidence or self-concept?

Read **Isaiah 43:1–2**. What do these words tell us about how God views us?

Read **Romans 5:1–8**. How, according to these verses, has God proven His love for us?

Can you imagine such a God not caring for those whom He has redeemed by the blood of His only-begotten Son, Jesus Christ? He has cured our greatest "disability"—our fatal sin sickness—through Christ. No matter what we may face, God loves us. He hears our prayers and answers them with "yes," "not now," or "I've got a better idea." We can trust that He will act for our good and according to His will.

INTO THE WORD

Read **Mark 1:40–45** and respond to these questions:

1. What words indicate that the man with leprosy believed in Jesus' divine power?

2. Why did Jesus heal this man?

3. Why do you think Jesus told the man not to tell anyone about this healing? What does the man do?

4. Read **2 Corinthians 12:7–10**. God does not always answer prayer with healing. How else can His glory be seen in adversity?

WHAT'S YOUR ISSUE?

What prevents young people who are struggling with problems from confidently taking them to Jesus as did the man who had leprosy? (See **Matthew 11:28–29**.)

What struggles or problems do *you* need to talk with God about?

Created in Christ © 2006 Concordia Publishing House. Reproduced by permission.

42. Forgiveness—The Greatest Miracle!

Mark 2:1–12

Lesson Focus

The paralytic was healed as proof that Christ forgave his sins. Likewise, the greatest miracle of God's love for us is proven in His Son's death and resurrection for the forgiveness of all our sins.

OPENING (5 minutes)

Pass out a sheet of paper to each student and ask students to write what they think was the greatest miracle in the Bible. When they are done, invite them to share their answers and why they chose that miracle. Ask students what one thing all these miracles have in common. (God made them all happen.) Hold up your sheet of paper on which is written "FORGIVENESS OF SINS." God performed all these miracles to point us to Jesus as the Savior of the world. That is why our forgiveness in Christ is God's greatest miracle!

GETTING INTO SCRIPTURE (15 minutes)

Distribute copies of Student Page 42. Have the students read Mark 2:1–5. The man needed to walk, to get close enough to Jesus for healing, and to have the assurance his sins were forgiven. The Lord had blessed this man with good friends who creatively "went through the roof"! Jesus saw faith in all of their hearts. Our Lord knows the most important need we have—the forgiveness of sins—so He said, "Son, your sins are forgiven."

GOING DEEPER (15 minutes)

Read Mark 2:6–7. Guide a discussion of the questions on the student page.

The "invisible problem" following Jesus' word of forgiveness to the paralytic began to unfold in the minds of the Jewish religious leaders who were there. They did not believe Jesus was God's Son. They accused Him of blaspheming (making fun of God, belittling Him) by forgiving sins—which only God can do. Jesus could read their minds! It is important for us to remember that God knows everything we think too! Jesus told the man, "Get up, take your mat and go home," which he did. Jesus forgave the man his sins. This is the greatest miracle because it brings everlasting life.

PONDERING THE GOSPEL (15 minutes)

Just as Jesus had the power to heal the paralytic, so Jesus proved He also has His Father's authority on earth to forgive the sins of all who believe. Through the mercy of God, Jesus died on the cross to pay for our sins once and for all through His blood. In our Baptism the Holy Spirit gave us saving faith in Jesus and daily washes away our sins—renewing us in that faith and life with God! See if the students can relate any "miracle stories" they know. Point out that God always receives the credit for our help, even when people are His "tools."

CLOSING (5 minutes)

Together, recite the Apostles' Creed. Follow with a prayer thanking God for His merciful love in Jesus and His greatest miracle—our forgiveness, which He won by His suffering and death.

LESSON EXTENDERS

✝ See John 20:21–23. When Jesus rose from the dead, what authority did He give to His church on earth? (To forgive sins) Who pronounces that forgiveness to us in the worship service? (The pastor)

✝ See Ephesians 4:32. Why should we be "kind and compassionate . . . forgiving each other"?

Forgiveness—The Greatest Miracle!

GETTING INTO SCRIPTURE

Read **Mark 2:1–5**. Miracles are special acts God performs that are impossible for us to do. They are signs of God's power and make us marvel at Him. In these verses, how did the man need help

• in his body?

....

• in getting to Jesus?

....

• in his relationship with God?

....

How did the man receive help getting to Jesus?

....

What did Jesus see when He looked at the man?

....

What was the first need Jesus took care of in the man's life?

....

....

GOING DEEPER

Read **Mark 2:6–7**. What invisible problem developed for Jesus?

Now read **Mark 2:8–12**. What miracles happened:

• regarding this "invisible" problem?

....

• regarding this man's "body" problem?

....

• regarding this man's "relationship with God" problem?

....

....

PONDERING THE GOSPEL

Share your reflections on the thoughts below.

The miracle Jesus performed on the man in today's lesson amazed all who were there. What very important connection did Jesus make between the miracle performed on the man's body and the man's relationship with God?

....

....

God performed the same miracle on us and continues this miracle in us every day! See **Titus 3:4–7**. How does Jesus work this greatest miracle in our life today?

....

....

God still performs miracles today, although He uses people and the gifts He gives as instruments through which He performs many of these miracles. Can you share any specific stories where God has performed a miracle for you or someone you know?

....

....

STUDENT PAGE 42

Created in Christ © 2006 Concordia Publishing House. Reproduced by permission.

43. HE'S ALL THAT!

Luke 4:14–32

Lesson Focus

Teens are trying to figure out what kind of career, spouse, car, and lifestyle they need to make life complete. The purpose of this study is to help them see that a personal relationship with Jesus Christ guarantees everything they really need.

WHAT IF? (15 minutes)

Distribute copies of Student Page 43. Ask students to describe in the box their idea of a perfect life. When they are finished have them share their concepts, listing them on the board.

Then ask, "Which of the things listed might you lose if you were disabled and couldn't work anymore?" Direct students to cross off those things in their descriptions that other students mention, as you cross them off the master list. "How about the death of a spouse or children?" Ask them to cross off those items that include family. "What if war or a huge natural disaster destroyed your town?" Tell students to cross off all of the material items on their lists. Challenge your students with this question: "If a perfect life depends on these things, what happens when they are lost? Would joy and contentment be impossible?" Allow students to share their thoughts. Say, "Today we want to consider what really makes life complete."

LIFE WITH JESUS (25 minutes)

Direct a student to read Luke 4:14–32. Ask students to complete the table on their sheets by giving examples of people in need today. Then ask them to list specific examples of how Jesus helps such people in the world today. (For example, "those in prison" might be anyone enslaved by an addiction or sin. Jesus helps by providing forgiveness and freedom from sin as well as resources to overcome addiction.) After completing the table, invite students to share their ideas. Ask what role God has prepared for the church and Christians to play in helping people today.

IN MY LIFE (10 minutes)

Invite students to complete the phrase in the space on the student page. Have students share their answers. Conclude by having students pray for the person on their left that Jesus would help that person with their need.

THE BOTTOM LINE (5 minutes)

Conclude the lesson by reminding students that a complete life is not found in material things or situations that can change. A complete life is found in the forgiveness of our sins and the new life given to us through the death and resurrection of Jesus Christ. At the bottom of the student page is a scrambled sentence. Challenge students to unscramble it to see a modern "proverb" based on John 14:6 (*Jesus is life. All the rest is detail*).

LESSON EXTENDERS

- Invite students to make a bumper sticker with the "proverb" on it and place it on a school notebook or inside their locker.
- Ask students to think of ways their friends need to hear the Good News, be set free, have their sight restored, or be released from oppression. Challenge them to pray for these friends and look for ways to serve them in Jesus' name.

He's All That!

WHAT IF?

In the box below, describe what you think a perfect life would include.

IN MY LIFE

Where I need Jesus in my life right now is . . .

LIFE WITH JESUS

Read **Luke 4:14–32**. Next to each phrase below, list people today whom you would think Jesus is referring to.

	When the Messiah Came	Contemporary Counterparts	How Does It Happen Today?
Good news for the poor			
Freedom for prisoners			
Recovery of sight for the blind			
Release for the oppressed			

THE BOTTOM LINE

ussje si fiel. lal het ster si deilat

Created in Christ © 2006 Concordia Publishing House. Reproduced by permission.

44. Practical Parables

Matthew 13:31–50

Lesson Focus

Through parables about the kingdom of God, we are renewed in God's grace and empowered by Him to participate in His Kingdom.

PARABOLIC THINKING (10 minutes)

Write the following sayings (but not their meanings) on newsprint or on the board, *omitting* the italicized word or words. Have students guess the missing word(s) and explain the sayings.

- You can lead a *horse* to water, but you can't make it drink. (Personal responsibility is needed in all things.)
- *Hindsight* is better than *foresight*. (We never know what the future holds.)
- Throw *caution* to the wind. (Take a risk without concern for consequences.)
- Bite the *bullet*. (Tolerate temporary pain for a good result.)
- When it rains, it *pours*. (Many bad things often come at the same time.)

Then say, "These sayings are 'shorthand' expressions of earthly truths. Jesus often taught in parables, 'shorthand' expressions of the spiritual truths of His Word. Today we're going to examine several parables to discover the Good News they reveal to us."

PONDERING PARABLES (25 minutes)

Create four groups of students. Hand out copies of Student Page 44. Assign each group one of the four sections from the student page. After about fifteen minutes, have each group report. Incorporate the following in your discussion:

A. In the seed, the soil's nutrients and the sun's energy combine to create a tree. Yeast creates bubbles in dough to make bread rise. God nurtures the church and individual hearts through the power of the Gospel.

B. The Gospel seed planted by God the sower creates wheat (righteous people) who may be visibly indistinguishable from the weeds (unbelievers) planted by Satan. At the harvest (Judgment Day), the weeds and wheat will be separated by God's wisdom, according to faith not works.

C. These parables illustrate the value of God's kingdom. God's grace is priceless; we cannot buy it. Those without faith will not understand the Christian's motivations in daily life.

D. The net is the world full of good and bad fish—righteous and unrighteous people. On heavenly shores, God will sort His catch, on the basis not of our works, but of faith in His Son, Jesus Christ. (See Ephesians 2:8–9.)

PUTTING PARABLES TO WORK (15 minutes)

Have the students discuss what they would do in each situation, referring to the previous discussions.

Situation A hint: God is in Billy spreading His kingdom. Billy has great potential because of the power of the cross.

Situation B hint: God is not only a righteous judge. He loves us, knows our needs, and forgives us.

Situation C hint: Christians find joy in whatever role God gives, not in earthly things. "He who dies with the most toys" still dies.

Situation D hint: God loved us "while we were sinners" (Romans 5:8). Forgiven through Christ, we share His love with others—not because we are perfect, but because we want them to share in forgiveness and new life.

CLOSING (5 minutes)

Read Matthew 13:35. Jesus taught these parables so that we could understand the deep truths of God! Invite each person to thank God for one thing they've learned from these parables and for strength to live out these truths.

LESSON EXTENDERS

✝ Review other parables that the students remember.

Practical Parables

Read these parables Jesus teaches in **Matthew 13** and discuss the questions in each section below.

Warm-up: Share a dream that became reality, a hidden talent someone suggested you pursue, or something that started out small and became a big success.

Dig in: Read **Matthew 13:31–35**. Why can large trees grow from small seeds? What does yeast contribute to bread? Jesus began with twelve disciples; today over a billion people claim to be Christians. How does this reflect this parable?

Reflect: How can the church or your faith be like the mustard seed or yeast?

Warm-up: If you were to clean your room or locker, what would be kept? What would be thrown away? How would you decide?

Dig in: Read **Matthew 13:36–43** (see also verses **24–29**). Who do these parts of the parable represent: the seeds? the weeds? the sower? the enemy? the harvest? the harvester? the fire? What's the point of this parable?

Reflect: Christians sin. Does that mean that God will weed out Christians also?

Warm-up: What is the most valuable thing that you own? Your house is on fire; you can only save four things. What would you save and why?

Dig in: Read **Matthew 13:44–46**. Under what circumstances do the actions of the man and the merchant make sense? Why do the actions of Christians appear foolish to those who are not Christian?

Reflect: Would you be willing to give up your most valuable possession for the kingdom of God?

Warm-up: In your opinion, what's the difference between good and bad people? Are a person's values always apparent by observation?

Dig in: Read **Matthew 13:47–51**. What does the net represent in this parable? Who is the fisherman? Why and on what basis does he sort the catch?

Reflect: In God's eyes, who are the good fish and bad fish? (Use Bible verses to explain your answers.)

PUTTING PARABLES TO WORK

Situation A: Billy, a guy in your youth group, is sort of a nerd. He isn't very popular, but he loves God and is always willing to help others. How might you defend Billy when others bad-mouth him?

Situation B: Your world religions class is discussing "heaven and hell" and a final judgment. Some students say a righteous, judgmental God is out of touch with reality. What do you share with them?

Situation C: Many of your friends see a big income as the reason for choosing a career. They think happiness is based on what you have! What would you say to them about money and possessions?

Situation D: Your friends say that since you aren't perfect, you have no right to criticize their actions. How do you face yourself, your friends, and God knowing that you have sinned?

Created in Christ © 2006 Concordia Publishing House. Reproduced by permission.

45. ONE THING NEEDED

Luke 10:38–42

Lesson Focus

We often push God out of our lives with busyness and activities, but God desires us to find comfort and peace in His loving arms, in the embrace of the church, and in His Word.

TOUGH CHOICES (10 minutes)

Copy and distribute Student Page 45. Discuss the questions from the survey and students' responses. Help them to understand their own decision-making processes as they sort through the questions.

THE BETTER CHOICE (20 minutes)

Have students read Luke 10:38–42 and Matthew 6:25–27. Discuss the questions regarding these verses as a whole group. Point out that Martha's choice to work in the kitchen wouldn't ordinarily be wrong; however, she chose the wrong thing at the wrong time. Mary's lack of assistance could be construed as laziness; however, Jesus applauds her devotion while chastising Martha. Discuss how this relates to the choices young people make.

Read Psalm 27:4 together with students. This verse reminds us that we need to focus on Christ. When we gather to worship Christ, the focus is no longer on us, but on God.

GOD CHOOSES US (15 minutes)

Encourage students to find comfort in the saving work of Jesus—even when their bad choices have disrupted their relationship with Him. Romans 8:1–4 comforts the reader with the reassuring message of the Gospel. Even when we are sinful and self-absorbed, Christ offers us His free grace and forgiveness. Give students the opportunity to share other encouraging Bible verses they think about when they are struggling or need to make an important decision. Give students time to write out their selected verse on a 3 x 5-inch card.

CLOSING (5 minutes)

Use the closing hymn, "Christ Be My Leader" (*LSB* 861, *LW* 365), as a prayer for the students. Help them recognize that with Jesus as our focus, our life is truly blessed with the "one thing needful."

LESSON EXTENDERS

✝ Consider looking at the more difficult hymn, "One Thing's Needful" (*LSB* 536, *LW* 277). Challenge students to find references to the Luke 10 text studied in the lesson.

ONE THING NEEDED

TOUGH CHOICES

Which would you choose and why?

Confirmation day or an out-of-town championship game?

....

Youth Bible study or a concert at school?

....

Sleeping in or going to church?

....

Can you think of other instances when you have to make choices between God and other activities?

....

THE BETTER CHOICE

Read **Luke 10:38–42** and **Matthew 6:25–27**. What was Martha doing?

....

What is accomplished by worrying?

....

When you worry, who are you making more important—yourself or God?

....

What is something you're worrying about right now?

....

Read **Psalm 27:4**. What was Mary doing?

....

What is accomplished by worship?

....

When you worship, who is doing the serving—yourself or God?

....

What is preventing you from worship now?

....

GOD CHOOSES US

We will sometimes—even often—make bad choices. We ignore God, and try to push Him out of our lives. But it is while we are sinners that God comes to us, forgiving and loving us, inviting us to be in His presence and receive His good gifts.

Read **Romans 8:1–4**. How do these verses encourage you?

....

....

....

....

On a 3 x 5-inch card write out a verse from the Bible that encourages you in your faith. Carry this Bible passage in your pocket to remind you that God's Word is effective, and He works in you to help you choose the best path.

Consider these verses if you have trouble finding your own:

Matthew 6:25

Luke 10:41–42

James 5:8

Psalm 13:5–6

STUDENT PAGE 45

Created in Christ © 2006 Concordia Publishing House. Reproduced by permission.

46. Change-Up

Matthew 17:1–9

Lesson Focus

Christ is the fulfillment of the Law and the Prophets (the prophecies). Christ's love for us, demonstrated most completely in His death and resurrection, is unchanging, even in the face of change.

CHANGING LANES
(15 minutes)

Hand out copies of Student Page 46. Change is difficult for everyone. Sometimes we decide to make a change; other changes are forced upon us. Give examples from your own life of both good and bad changes that you had to make, including, if possible, what precipitated those changes and then the results. Encourage your students to share as well.

The transfiguration of Christ takes place at the halfway point of Jesus' ministry, between temptation and Gethsemane. The change in His physical appearance serves to encourage the disciples who will now join their Master on the long road to Jerusalem, a road that will eventually culminate in Jesus' suffering and death. The disciples are not without fear, and they are certainly in denial of this eventuality. Peter vehemently opposes it. Therefore, this glimpse of the glorified Christ is a foretaste of the feast to come, for with His death and resurrection the change from old to new covenant is complete.

PITCHING CHANGE
(20 minutes)

In baseball, near the end of the game, the manager of the team that's winning may call for his closing pitcher to come in and continue the good work of the previous pitchers and secure the victory.

Moses the lawgiver and Elijah the prophet being present on the mount illustrates that Jesus is the fulfillment of both the Law and the Prophets. You may wish to point out that both Moses and Elijah began a good work and then were taken up by God, who then left someone special behind to complete the work. Joshua ("the LORD saves") replaced Moses, and Elisha, whose name is another form of Joshua, replaced Elijah. Jesus, or Yeshua, again a form of Joshua, who came to be the completion of all that had begun, "replaced" John the Baptizer. Many at that time believed that John was Elijah, foretold by Malachi (4:5–6) as reappearing before the coming of the Messiah. Jesus Himself makes this reference in Matthew 11:14.

The disciples hid their faces in fear and awe at the sound of God's voice. When they raised their heads, Moses and Elijah were gone. Jesus alone can complete our salvation, and to Him only we turn our faces, even as He turned His toward Jerusalem.

Jesus is our closer. Not only does He complete the work begun by the Law and the Prophets, but He also secured for us the victory. For background, Hebrews 3 gives a comparison between Moses and Jesus. Hebrews 7:24–27 summarizes how the victory was won.

KEEP THE CHANGE
(15 minutes)

Now that Christ has won the victory for us, how can we keep the change that has come over us? Hebrews 12:1–3 offers some insight into that. Brainstorm other ways that we can keep the change. We are fed and kept by God by going to church, hearing and reading His Word, and receiving Holy Communion.

CLOSING (5 minutes)

Pray Hebrews 13:20–21 together, and sing "How Good, Lord, to Be Here" (*LW* 89).

CHANGE-UP

CHANGING LANES

In order to get where they're going, drivers often change lanes. In life, we too make changes to get where we're going. What changes have you had to make?

....

....

Read **Matthew 17:1–9**. What change did Peter, James, and John witness?

....

....

PITCHING CHANGE

Read **Malachi 4:5–6**. Why were Moses and Elijah on the mountain with Jesus?

....

....

The disciples hid their faces in fear. When they looked again, Moses and Elijah were gone. According to **Hebrews 3:1**, to whom are we supposed to look?

....

....

In what ways does Jesus secure the victory and complete the work done by Moses and the prophets (**Hebrews 7:24–27**)?

....

....

KEEP THE CHANGE

When the disciples saw the transfiguration of Christ, they changed too. Their faith was strengthened for the perilous road ahead. Read **Hebrews 12:1–3**. How can we keep the change?

....

Created in Christ © 2006 Concordia Publishing House. Reproduced by permission.

47. Building Up Your Strength

Luke 22:7–38;
Mark 9:24;
John 6:37;
1 John 1:7

Lesson Focus

Communion is a sacrament given to us by Jesus Christ for the strengthening of our faith. By the grace of God, the students will see Communion as a way God builds strong faith in their lives.

OPENING (10 minutes)

Ask, "If you could take something that would make you stronger, smarter, or more attractive, would you do it? Why or why not? Do you know anything like that? Today we will explore how the Lord's Supper can make our faith stronger."

THE ISSUE (10 minutes)

Distribute copies of Student Page 47. Have students check all the things they think or feel when they take Communion. Invite volunteers to share their responses, explaining why they chose the words they did.

THE WORD (20 minutes)

As you read Luke 22:7–38, have the students follow along and underline words that indicate power or strength for them. Discuss students' choices.

In groups, have students look up the other three passages. Have each group write what the passage says about making their faith strong.

THE WORLD (10 minutes)

Encourage the students to thoughtfully write an ending to the sentences. Allow volunteers to share answers. Reflect on what it is that God has given us in the Lord's Supper to keep our faith strong.

CLOSING (5 minutes)

Have the students stand in a circle and, if they are willing, hold hands. Pray, or let the students pray, offering thanks to God for providing the Lord's Supper as a gift that strengthens our faith. Ask God to strengthen each of you the next time you share in His holy meal together.

LESSON EXTENDERS

✝ Review the sections about Communion in *Luther's Small Catechism with Explanation*. Read either Luther's questions and answers or questions 296–304.

✝ Have students interview members of the congregation, asking them why or how the Lord's Supper strengthens their faith. Or have your class members interview students preparing for their first Communion, asking why they are looking forward to participating in the Sacrament. Use a video camera, if appropriate, to record answers.

Building Up Your Strength

THE ISSUE

What do you feel or think when you attend the Lord's Supper?

Joy

Fear

Love

Closeness to God

Solemnity

Sadness

Strength

Power

Wonder

Commitment

....
....
....
....
....
....

THE WORD

Jesus institutes (that is, celebrates for the first time) the Sacrament of Communion in **Luke 22:7–38**. Read the passage, underlining the words that indicate power or strength for you.

What do the following have to say about making your faith strong?

Mark 9:24

....

John 6:37

....

1 John 1:7

....

THE WORLD

I am weak spiritually . . .

....

....

The Lord's Supper gives me strength . . .

....

....

My faith is made strong . . .

....

....

STUDENT PAGE 47

48. THE MOST AMAZING STORY EVER TOLD

Matthew 27:27–66

Lesson Focus

In His Word, God lays out the most amazing story ever told—the story of His love for us and His plan to save us from our sin.

INTRODUCTION (10 minutes)

Ask students to share the title of a book they have read, a movie they've seen, or a story they have enjoyed hearing more than once. After students have shared, ask what keeps them interested even though they know the ending.

Tell students that today they are going to focus on a story they have probably heard before. But since it is the best story ever told, it's worth hearing over and over again!

Open with a prayer asking the Holy Spirit to make this most amazing story come alive for each person involved in this study today.

THE VILLAIN ENTERS THE SCENE (10 minutes)

Distribute copies of Student Page 48. Ask everyone to read Romans 5:12 and 19 to discover the villain. Make sure students understand that the villain is sin.

Ask three volunteers to read the passages aloud. Discuss together the three key facts: we are sinful from conception; sin separates us from God; a sinner's mind is hostile to God.

HUMAN ATTEMPTS TO OVERCOME THE VILLAIN (5 minutes)

Ask volunteers to read aloud one of the passages. After the passages are read, ask students to discuss the questions together. Each passage indicates that humans have tried to work their way back to a relationship with God. However, this is impossible since people can't keep God's commands. We become boastful or filled with pride over the laws we do keep.

GOD TO THE RESCUE! (10 minutes)

Ask volunteers to read aloud a passage from the student page. After each reading have students discuss God's rescue plan. Guide students to understand these points: 2 Corinthians 5:21—God placed our sin on One who was sinless (Jesus). Galatians 3:13—We were condemned to a life separated from God and to eternal death because we broke the Law, but Christ has taken that condemnation upon Himself. Hebrews 2:17—Christ became human to minister to people and to pay the debt created by our sin. 1 Peter 2:24—Christ took our sin upon Himself in order to set us free from the power of sin and sin's ability to control us.

A HAPPY ENDING (5 minutes)

Ask volunteers to read aloud a passage; discuss each passage after it is read. Students should see that believers receive eternal life and become new creatures who, because they are now holy and without the blemish of sin, are no longer separated from God but are reconciled to Him.

CLOSING (10 minutes)

Provide time for students to quietly reflect on the familiar story of Christ's death and resurrection recorded in Matthew 27:32–28:10 and on what it means for them. You may want to find some appropriate music to play while students meditate on God's Word. Close with prayer.

THE MOST AMAZING STORY EVER TOLD

THE VILLAIN ENTERS THE SCENE

Read **Romans 5:12** and **19** to discover the villain.

Read the following passages to see how the villain affects our relationship with God.

Psalm 5:4–5

....

....

Isaiah 59:2

....

....

Romans 8:7

....

....

HUMAN ATTEMPTS TO OVERCOME THE VILLAIN

What do the following passages imply about how humans have attempted to solve the problem of sin? How successful are they?

Galatians 3:10

....

....

James 2:10

....

....

Ephesians 2:9

....

....

GOD TO THE RESCUE!

Read the following passages and consider God's plan for assuring that the villain doesn't win out over us.

2 Corinthians 5:21

....

Galatians 3:13

....

Hebrews 2:17

....

1 Peter 2:24

....

A HAPPY ENDING

Read these passages to see what happens to believers.

John 3:16

....

2 Corinthians 5:17–19

....

Colossians 1:22

....

Created in Christ © 2006 Concordia Publishing House. Reproduced by permission.

STUDENT PAGE 48

49. More Than Easter

Luke 24:1–11;
Matthew 28:1–10;
1 Corinthians 15:1–11

Lesson Focus

Students will be familiar with Easter and its trappings. In this lesson they review the real meaning of Easter and consider what the resurrection of Jesus means to them.

OPENING (10 minutes)

Write the words *peace*, *love*, and *hope* on the board or on a piece of paper. Ask, "Which do you think is easiest to find: real peace, real love, or real hope? Why? Why are each of these difficult to find? How do people look for them in the wrong places? What can happen to people who 'have no hope'?"

EASTER AND MORE (10 minutes)

Bring some Easter things—flowers, colorful eggs, and butterfly pictures—to class. Or ask students to draw or describe some of the things we normally associate with Easter on their copy of Student Page 49. Discuss: "What does this stuff mean? What do you think it means out in the world? What does it say to you? What do these things have to do with resurrection?"

INTO THE WORD (20 minutes)

Ask students to work together to recall and tell the real Easter story. They might work in pairs and write down the details they remember. After a few minutes, invite volunteers to share their work.

Read aloud, or have volunteers read aloud, Luke 24:1–11 and Matthew 28:1–10. Compare the accounts with what the students recalled, listing the things that happened.

Ask, "What do you think that first Easter meant to the women? to the disciples? When do you think they really understood what happened on that morning?"

Have students read 1 Corinthians 15:1–11 and answer the questions on the student page. After allowing them to work for a while, bring the group together to share and discuss their answers.

BRINGING IT HOME (10 minutes)

Ask students to respond to the questions on the student page. Ask volunteers to read what they have written.

Discuss what the resurrection of Jesus has to do with

- His death;
- the death of our loved ones;
- our own death;
- our hope of new life.

Invite the students to look again at the Easter items that you brought or that they drew. Ask, "How can these symbols of Easter bring to mind the real story and meaning of Easter? How can they help us remember and tell the story of the resurrection?"

CLOSING (5 minutes)

Sing together an Easter hymn. Ask a volunteer to offer a prayer asking the Spirit to renew the students' hope in the resurrection.

LESSON EXTENDERS

✝ Suggest the students carry and give away simple Easter objects (flowers, chocolate rabbits, colored eggs) this week. As they give, they might share the Easter story. Talk about their experience at your next session.

✝ Ask students to write a letter of hope to someone who is grieving or lonely. They might write the letter to themselves to save to read when they feel lost and lonely. Those who are willing might share their letters.

More Than Easter

EASTER AND MORE

Draw some of the symbols of Easter.

What do these things have to do with the Easter resurrection of Jesus?

INTO THE WORD

What specific details do you remember about the first Easter? Who visited the tomb? In what order? How did they react? Why? (Check out **Luke 24:1–11** if you need help.)

Read **1 Corinthians 15:1–11**.

What does Paul tell us is the meaning of that `first Easter?

What does it mean about our own death?

What can we hope for?

BRINGING IT HOME

What does Easter mean to you?

Created in Christ © 2006 Concordia Publishing House. Reproduced by permission.

50. No Doubt About It

John 20:19–31

Lesson Focus

As the Bible testifies, God works in our lives daily to help us know and trust Him with absolute certainty.

OPENING (5 minutes)

Have students work with partners to list things they believed in when they were younger. (Santa Claus, the Easter Bunny, and the Tooth Fairy are possible responses.) Have volunteers share their responses. Ask, "When did you first doubt these things? What changed your beliefs?"

DOUBT CHECKLIST (5 minutes)

Distribute copies of Student Page 50. Have the students mark the checklist. Assure them they won't be required to share their answers.

DOUBTING DISCIPLES (20 minutes)

Have students follow along as a volunteer reads John 20:19–31 aloud. Discuss the student page questions, using these comments to clarify the issues. (1) The disciples were in hiding; they doubted God's ability to protect them from those who crucified their Lord. (2) Jesus reassures them in three ways—with His words ("Peace"), actions (showing proof of His identity), and commission ("I am sending you"). (3) Thomas may have felt slighted for missing out on the other disciples' experience. (4) Jesus reassures Thomas also with His words, actions, and commission (assumed). (5) Most of the people in John's Gospel did see the resurrected Christ. John must have sensed that his account of Christ's life would be shared with others. Verse 31 is specific—people come to faith through reading and hearing the words about Jesus in the Scriptures.

GOD'S ANSWER TO DOUBT (15 minutes)

Direct students to mark responses in this section of the student page that would be a good response to doubt. Point out that answers (a), (b), and (c) would not be effective ways to respond to spiritual doubts. Denying doubt, feeling guilty, and just hoping it will go away may *foster* doubt because those responses focus on ourselves. Answer (d) could be helpful if the person consulted directs the doubter to God and His Word. Answers (e), (f), and (g) are the best responses. Our faith is strengthened not by anything we do, but by what God has done and is doing for us. He has given us the Holy Spirit, who works through the Word to focus us on Him.

Have the students look again at the "Doubt Checklist." Point out that, just as Jesus told Thomas to "stop doubting and believe," it is God's desire that we completely trust Him. On our own, we are incapable of believing any of the items on this list. But through His Word and with the help of the Holy Spirit, we can know all the items on the checklist with complete confidence.

CLOSING (5 minutes)

Close with a prayer like this one: "We admit, Lord, that we have given in to doubt. Forgive us for our lack of faith. Send your Spirit to keep us focused, not on ourselves, but on who You are and what You have done for us through Jesus Christ. Amen."

LESSON EXTENDERS

✝ In Mark 9:24, a man says to Jesus, "I do believe; help me overcome my unbelief!" How do our lives reflect this man's situation? How does God respond?

✝ How would you advise a Christian friend who confesses experiencing doubts in his or her spiritual life?

No Doubt About It

DOUBT CHECKLIST

Do you ever doubt that . . .

- ☐ God actually knows you?
- ☐ your life matters to anyone?
- ☐ the Bible is true?
- ☐ God hears your prayers?
- ☐ God really exists?
- ☐ Jesus lived, died, and rose again?
- ☐ you will go to heaven when you die?

DOUBTING DISCIPLES

Thomas is the disciple who is most frequently called "doubting." As you read **John 20:19–31**, note the indications that the other disciples had their doubts as well.

1. What indications do you find that the other disciples had their doubts after the crucifixion? What specifically do you think they doubted God could or would do?

2. How does Jesus reassure the disciples of His love and power? (Look for three ways.)

3. What might be a reason for Thomas's persistent doubt despite his fellow disciples' testimony about Jesus' resurrection?

4. How does Jesus deal with Thomas's doubt?

5. Read again **John 20:29–31**. Whom do you think John means by "those who have not seen"? How do those who are not eyewitnesses to Jesus' life, death, and resurrection come to faith?

GOD'S ANSWER TO DOUBT

When your faith is challenged by doubt, should you (mark all that apply)

a. __ try not to think about it?

b. __ feel guilty?

c. __ hope it goes away?

d. __ talk to someone about it?

e. __ pray, asking God for help?

f. __ seek encouragement by reading your Bible?

g. __ focus on Christ—what He has done and is doing for you?

Created in Christ © 2006 Concordia Publishing House. Reproduced by permission.

51. WHAT'S THE PLAN?

Acts 1:1–11

Lesson Focus

Because of Jesus' death and resurrection, we can plan to live in heaven when we die. God empowers us by the Holy Spirit to tell others of His plan of salvation.

PLANNING MY WAY (5 minutes)

Distribute copies of Student Page 51. Allow students time to mark their preference on the chart. As an alternative, encourage students to move about the room by saying, "Imagine that the left corner is 'I've got to have things planned all the time' and the right corner is 'I'll figure it out when the time comes.' Move to where you would most likely be." Ask, "Can you think of a time when planning is essential? Can you imagine a time when you would be more successful without a plan?"

LOOKING FOR THE PLANS (20 minutes)

Ask a volunteer to read Acts 1:1–11. Discuss the questions together, referring to the text when necessary. Emphasize that Jesus' life and death were not unplanned. They are part of God's eternal plan to place the punishment for our sins on Jesus so we can be forgiven and live forever in heaven with Him. Jesus' resurrection proves His victory over sin, death, and the devil. He sends His Spirit to empower us to spread this news to others. When the time is right, He will return to take all who trust Him as their Savior to heaven to live with Him. We know that God's plan was also to send all disciples into the world with the message of God's love and forgiveness in Christ.

A WORD ABOUT PLANNING (15 minutes)

Encourage students to share their short- and long-term plans. Read the Bible passages together. Ask, "What promises does God make in these verses? Are your plans compatible with what God asks you to do?" Emphasize that God knows what is best for us and brings about good, even if it is not what we wish for ourselves.

LET'S MAKE A PLAN (10 minutes)

We proclaim God's transforming love plan when we

live in peace with our family and friends at home;

are grateful for our many blessings;

gather for worship and church activities, singing His praises;

study God's Word so we can teach and admonish others;

say and do things that honor God.

Remind students that people will want to know more about Jesus when they observe our faith in action.

CLOSING (5 minutes)

If you haven't already done so, share plans that you (the leader) have made to witness to others. Read Hebrews 13:20–21 as a closing blessing. Pray for specific concerns raised during the lesson. Especially ask the Holy Spirit to help motivate and empower His children to speak for Jesus. If time allows, sing or pray together "Draw Us to You" (*LSB* 701, *LW* 153).

LESSON EXTENDERS

✝ What else does the Bible say about planning to be a witness? See Luke 14:25–33. When might it be necessary to give up popularity, financial gain, or comfort to tell others about Jesus? How can the Holy Spirit help you?

What's the Plan?

PLANNING MY WAY

Are you more likely to . . .

- ☐ Study for Monday's test on Friday? . . . . Cram for a test right before you take it? ☐
- ☐ Shop around to get the best buys? . . . . Spend your earnings on the first thing you see? ☐
- ☐ Save your money for college? . . . . Hope for a scholarship? ☐
- ☐ Look for a summer job during Christmas vacation? . . . . Worry about it when the time comes? ☐

LOOKING FOR THE PLANS

Read **Acts 1:1–11** and answer the questions.

Verses 1–2: What plan did the author have for his first book (probably Luke)?

Verse 3: What plan did Jesus follow in the days between His resurrection and ascension? How does this plan help us today?

Verses 4–5: What plan did Jesus ask the disciples to make?

Verses 6–7: What evidence is there that the disciples misunderstood Jesus' plan? In what ways do people still misunderstand Jesus today?

Verse 8: What plan did Jesus have for the disciples? How is this like His plans for us?

Verses 9–11: What is the plan for Jesus' return? Are you ready for this to happen?

A WORD ABOUT PLANNING

What plans do you have for the future?

What has God planned for you?

Jeremiah 29:11–13; Hebrews 13:20–21

LET'S MAKE A PLAN

How can you be a witness in . . . (See **Colossians 3:15–17** for help.)

your home?

your church?

your school?

your community?

STUDENT PAGE 51

Created in Christ © 2006 Concordia Publishing House. Reproduced by permission.

52. Pentecost Power

Acts 2:1–41

Lesson Focus

The gift of the Holy Spirit was given to the disciples at Pentecost to equip them for the work Jesus called them to do. The Holy Spirit is with us now in the work to which *we* are called.

ALL ALONE (10 minutes)

Distribute copies of Student Page 52. Give students a few minutes to complete the continuum activity. Discuss why they responded as they did. Most people are more likely to do daring things if they don't have to do them alone. The same is true for Christians. The difference is that Christians are never alone. We may not be called to bungee jump, but are called to do things that can sometimes seem scary.

THE "SECRET AGENT" SHOWS HIMSELF (5 minutes)

Work together as a whole group to read the text and answer the questions from this section. Before Jesus was taken up into heaven, He promised the disciples that they would be "baptized with the Holy Spirit" and that they would receive power when this happened (Acts 1:5–8). On the day of Pentecost the Holy Spirit came upon the disciples in very tangible ways. There was a violent wind, and tongues of fire rested on the disciples without burning them. The disciples also suddenly had the ability to speak many different languages that they didn't even know.

THE "AGENT" WORKING FOR THE DISCIPLES (15 minutes)

Allow pairs of students to work together to complete this section. Discuss their insights with the whole group. In the Great Commission Jesus commanded the disciples to "make disciples of all nations" by baptizing and teaching them. There was, however, a language barrier for the disciples. When the Holy Spirit came upon them, however, they were able to speak the languages they needed to speak the words they needed to say. They were truly inspired.

Pentecost itself was, in a way, a great kickoff for the Great Commission. The disciples were telling the Lord's message in a way they could not have done previously. Peter, especially, was bold and inspired by the Spirit. Consequently, "Those who accepted his message were baptized, and about three thousand were added to their number that day" (Acts 2:41).

THE "AGENT" WORKING FOR YOU (10 minutes)

Complete this section working as a whole group. In case one thinks that the Holy Spirit came to the disciples with just a one-time show at Pentecost, Acts 2:38–39 indicates otherwise. The Holy Spirit is for all who are baptized and believe. Verse 39 may have particular relevance because it promises the Spirit's presence for generations to come, including those today.

Discuss ways students may be called in their Christian walk. Emphasize that this can include things that seem big and things that seem small. Maybe it is a calling to begin preparation for full-time service in the church. Perhaps it is befriending the kid everyone else picks on. No matter what they are, callings can be accomplished through the power of the Holy Spirit.

CLOSING (10 minutes)

Spend time together in prayer thanking the Lord for the presence of His Holy Spirit and asking for the Spirit's power in recognizing and accomplishing the work of the Lord each day.

Pentecost Power

ALL ALONE

Place an X on the continuum to indicate how likely you would be to do each thing on your own. Place a star on the continuum to indicate how likely you would be to do that thing with a friend. Place a circle on the continuum to indicate how likely you would be to do each thing if you had a highly trained special agent with you.

Would you...

go bungee jumping? sure _____ no way

eat a chocolate-covered bug? sure _____ no way

travel to China? sure _____ no way

talk to a group of people about your faith? sure _____ no way

THE "SECRET AGENT" SHOWS HIMSELF

Read **Acts 2:1–13**.

What "Secret Agent" came on Pentecost?

....

How did the people know He was there?

....

THE "AGENT" WORKING FOR THE DISCIPLES

What had the disciples been called, even commanded, to do prior to Pentecost? (See **Matthew 28:18–20**.)

....

Considering the fact that most of the disciples didn't have much of an education, why might the command to "make disciples of all nations" be a particular challenge?

....

How did the Holy Spirit equip the disciples to meet the challenges of their call (**Acts 2:4**)?

....

Read **Acts 2:14–41**.

How did the Holy Spirit equip the disciples (especially Peter) for their work on Pentecost day itself?

....

What was the result of the Spirit-inspired words of Peter and the other disciples on the day of Pentecost?

....

THE "AGENT" WORKING FOR YOU

What encouraging promise do you have as a disciple of Christ (**Acts 2:38–39**)?

....

Where in your life is the Lord calling you to do His work through the power of the Holy Spirit?

....

Created in Christ © 2006 Concordia Publishing House. Reproduced by permission.

STUDENT PAGE 52

Property of

St. John Youth Squad

Donated by Becky Holman